Transcending the Game

Transcending the Game

Debate, Education, and Society

Edited by Shawn F. Briscoe

Southern Illinois University Press
Carbondale

Southern Illinois University Press
www.siupress.com

27 26 25 24   4 3 2 1

Cover illustration: Maya Desiree 2 by Ravi Rao. Image has
been cropped and colorized.

Library of Congress Cataloging-in-Publication Data
Names: Briscoe, Shawn F., editor.
Title: Transcending the game : debate, education, and society
/ edited by Shawn F. Briscoe.
Description: Carbondale : Southern Illinois University Press,
2023. | Includes bibliographical references and index. |
Identifiers: LCCN 2023014762 (print) |
LCCN 2023014763 (ebook) | ISBN 9780809339228 (paperback) |
ISBN 9780809339235 (ebook)
Subjects: LCSH: Debates and debating. | Social problems.
Classification: LCC PN4181 .T725 2023 (print) |
LCC PN4181 (ebook) | DDC 808.53—dc23/eng/20230623
LC record available at https://lccn.loc.gov/2023014762
LC ebook record available at https://lccn.loc.gov/2023014763

Printed on recycled paper ♻

SIU
Southern Illinois University System

Becky, Ben, and Hannah . . . more than the universe.

In loving memory
forever and for always
Debra Leivers
a wonderful Mom and Nana

Education . . . is not the art of putting the capacity of sight into the soul; the soul possesses that already but it is not turned the right way or looking where it should.

Plato, *The Republic*

Contents

Preface

> A person who deliberates . . . is inquiring into some-
> thing . . . Deliberation . . . is correctness . . . with respect
> to the right object, the right means and the right
> time . . . It is the mark of a prudent person to have delib-
> erated well.
>
> Aristotle, *Nicomachean Ethics*

We live in a world that would rather silence a disagreement by calling the other person a *loser*, a *snowflake*, a *libtard*, a *right-wing nutjob* or simply offering a condescending *we'll have to agree to disagree* or *good day* than have a meaningful conversation, hear the perspective of someone else, lend an empathetic ear, or engage in constructive dialogue. We tend toward a quick Google search, a meme, or cursory reading of headlines in place of research and understanding.

Today, more than ever, we must focus on structured debate that encourages one to hear the other side, challenges our assumptions, and builds toward something better. That venue exists within our secondary schools and post-secondary institutions. An extracurricular and co-curricular activity, academic debate fosters growth in the individual, with benefits not just for the participants, but for all society.

My involvement with academic, competitive debate spans over three decades. During that time, my experiences have been incredibly diverse. As a competitor, I was introduced to debate on the traditional and audience-friendly circuit in the southwest corner of Missouri. In college, I experienced a bit of whiplash as I entered the world of high speed, jargon-laced policy debate while at the United States Air Force Academy.

Over the years, I continued to work with students and coaches on audience-friendly circuits, the high school national circuit, urban debate league programs, and the international world of debate as practiced at the World Universities Debating Championships.

Despite their disparate approaches to the activity, I found that *good debate is good debate*, as the director of the Seawolf Debate Program, Steve Johnson, likes to say. While the styles, emphasis, and contestants themselves appear incredibly different, there is more that connects them than separates them. Regardless of the style embraced or approach taken, the activity has immeasurable benefits.

Throughout my time with these programs, I listened to non-debate educators disparage the activity as something devoid of merit. I observed rifts within the debate community that highlight the limitations of it. I witnessed the political and social discourse in our nation poison society. Nevertheless, I found that taken together, the unique approaches to the activity offer a path forward, a path of understanding, and a path of healing.

When examining the world of competitive debating, we clearly see three distinct stylistic approaches: audience-centered, progressive, and nontraditional. Different formats, circuits, and regions tend to preference one of these styles over the others. While radically different in their presentation, they all provide incredible value for participants.

To explore those benefits, I turned to individuals with a range of experience in competitive debating. At the high school level, many were immersed in policy, Lincoln- Douglas, student congress, public forum, and world schools debate. At the college level, contributors participated in formats such as the National Debate Tournament, Cross Examination Debate Association, National Parliamentary Debate Association, and British Parliamentary (or World Universities) debate.

That said, they all share a common background in policy debate.[1] I specifically sought contributors with some policy debate background because that format most clearly incorporates all three stylistic approaches. As a nexus for the three divergent perspectives on debate, it affords a unique look at why they exist, how they interact, and the insights they provide participants.

Debate is not perfect. It has shortcomings. It has room for improvement. Participants regularly highlight the disparities and inequalities that exist between programs and competitors. Even more accessible formats, such as British Parliamentary debate with its emphasis on public-facing discourse, have begun to confront these issues. At the 2021 United States Universities Debating Championships, Morehouse College withdrew from the national championship tournament after "they faced racist taunts from opposing teams" and their concerns went unaddressed in a timely manner.[2]

Despite significant improvement in equity and access, the activity (largely) remains the purview of white, economically privileged males.

To explore the benefits of the activity, I turned to individuals with diverse backgrounds. Some earned national championships. Some were midlevel debaters. Some are from rural areas, whereas others are from the suburbs or urban centers. Some competed for public schools and others private schools. Some come from places of relative wealth and others from poverty.

Some have lived the life of cisgender white males and the privilege that comes with it. Several identify as LGBTQIA. More than half are Black, Indigenous, and People of Color. More than half are women.

Hopefully, by drawing upon this diverse group of authors, you will find someone who speaks meaningfully to you and your students.

At times, I found it difficult to categorize authors within one stylistic approach. In truth, most of us have significant experience with multiple formats of debate and two or more stylistic approaches. When determining where to locate their chapters in the text, I made decisions based on their primary experience with the activity, what they considered to be their most meaningful involvement, or the specific theme of their chapter.

What follows is an immersive journey into the world of academic, competitive debate. This work grants insight into this unique activity and, by extension, our educational system. While the narratives paint, at times, diverging views of the activity, the net result is a glimpse at the profound impact the participants have on the activity and its impact upon them.

Notes

1. The obvious exceptions are Paul and Methanie Ongtooguk who do not have any debate background.

2. Eric Stirgus, "Morehouse Team Pulled Out of Debate Competition, Citing Racist Taunts," *Atlanta Journal Constitution*, April 29, 2021. https://www.ajc.com/education/morehouse-team-pulled-out-of-debate-competition-citing-racist-taunts/VUDNY3ZILFHMDNYOKYP43DYINU/.

Transcending the Game

Introduction

The prologue, "The Moment That Changed My Life," introduces readers to the world of competitive speech and debate through my personal journey—my introduction to this strange, unique, and transformative activity we call speech and debate. It operates outside an examination of academic debate by offering a personal account of what it means to be on a speech and debate team. Nevertheless, the narrative arc of that chapter explores elements that are recurring themes in essays throughout this book.

Section 1 establishes the foundations of the text. It highlights core elements of curricular debate within the discipline of communication, education, and society. The authors wrote generally about debate with lessons applicable across the spectrum of approaches. The section begins with Sara Sanchez's "Debate and Disinformation," in which she explores the state of civic discourse in America and how debate interacts with it.

Next, "Truth, A Casualty of Intellectual Warfare?" was my original inspiration for this anthology. It both dovetails with and extends the ideas explored in Sara's contribution.

In the third chapter, we change gears. Alex Berry takes a personal look at the role debate played in his life in the chapter "Finding Home." Beyond just academics, debate teams offer a socioemotional support network for students. His experience can be extrapolated to many students who struggle to find a place to call their own.

Finally, Aubrey Semple highlights the specific benefits debate provides when navigating the job market in his chapter "Putting Debate Skills to Work." Aubrey organizes his chapter into six pro tips for leveraging a debater's experiences when applying for jobs.

For additional readings on the nature of competitive debate, see this work's sister text, *Why Debate: Transformed by Academic Discourse*. The following chapters correlate to section 1 of *Transcending the Game*: Minh Luong's "A Guiding Force of History," Shawn F. Briscoe's "Debate Is," Kari Jahnsen's "Lasting Impressions," Shawn F. Briscoe's "Forensics: Enhancing Civic Literacy and Democracy," and Nicole Eldred's "Not a Team, but a Family."

In section 2, we explore the traditional roots of academic, competitive debate. Traditionally, debate was entrenched in rules that governed how students approached the activity and dictated how they interrogated topics. This perspective also prioritizes persuasive speaking skills in its audience-centered focus. Here, the authors show how participation in audience-centered discourse provides lasting benefits for the individual and our academic institutions.

The section begins with Gina Iberri-Shea's reflection in "Inspired Learning." She examines debate's traditional and audience-centered roots and how they benefit students of all types whether they are engineering students or English language learners. Additionally, she reflects on how debate made her a better educator and how participation acts as a force multiplier in educational institutions.

Her chapter is followed by Nya Fifer's "Debate and the College Experience." Nya writes from the perspective of an undergraduate student benefitting from her time in high school debate. She explores how her time in debate opened doors during the college application process, helped her navigate the dreaded college interview, and continues to have an impact on her undergraduate studies.

Next, "Around the World and Back Again" by Ashley Snookes traces her literal journey around the world and how debate sparked, enabled, and enhanced that voyage in discovery, experience, and career.

Finally, Ben Collinger takes a larger view in "Policy Debate in a Post-Modern Society." He examines the experience of debaters within the current political and social climate, and even goes so far as to identify some of the conflict present within the debate community itself.

For additional readings from the perspective of audience-centered debating, see this work's sister text, *Why Debate: Transformed by Academic Discourse*. The following chapters correlate to section 2 of *Transcending the Game*: Li Xi's "Adventures in Debate," Richard Omoniyi-Shoyoola's "The Speaker in Blue Agbada," Kenny Hubbell's "A Path to Adulthood," Jonathon Sanchez's "Trial by (Academic) Combat," Katy Bishoff's "A Debater's Philosophy of Teaching," Steven Johnson's "Debating in the Public Sphere," Sarah Garwood's "The Patient's Advocate," and Thomas D. Allison's "Breaking My Silence."

In section 3, we explore progressive movements within debate. These changes began in policy debate as early as the 1960s and had fully taken hold of the college debate circuit by the 1990s. This approach is most readily identified by and derided for its use of speed or talking at high rates of delivery. Although most would identify this approach by its fast rate of delivery, what really defines it is its progressive nature. Debaters immersed in this culture of debate experiment with stylistic deliveries, argument structures, content, and the theory or rules that define how the game is played. Consequently, it appears to be incredibly complex and difficult to access as the activity evolves.

While many consider this approach esoteric and removed from the world of education and the real world, the authors paint a different picture. Through their contributions, we see an activity that prepares participants to see the world in larger contexts, helps them navigate our political and economic world, and provides immeasurable benefits in our personal lives.

Section 3 begins with "Defending Policy Debate," in which I grapple with some of the criticisms that have been directed at the activity from coaches and educators as it has grown more complex, more technical, and increasingly fast-paced.

Next, Yari L. Mitchell's "Debate as a Framework for Business" identifies the practical applications of the activity. She highlights the similarities between debate and the business world. Specifically, she makes direct connections between competitive debate practices and their corresponding utility in her profession.

In "Engaging Each Other on the Merits of Our Arguments," Sean Luechtefeld discusses how debate prepares us to navigate a highly polarized world from disentangling claims to aid decision-making, to evaluating evidence and rhetorical efforts, and adapting our persuasive efforts to the audience before us.

Finally, Tara L. Tate takes us on an emotional ride in "A Mother's Journey from Debate to the NICU." She lays bare her family's upheaval when her daughter was born prematurely. She discusses how debate got her through the trauma, uncertainty, and so much more.

For additional readings from the perspective of contemporary, progressive debating, see this work's sister text, *Why Debate: Transformed by Academic Discourse*. The following chapters correlate to section 3 of *Transcending the Game*: Ryan Davis's "From Policy Debate to Project Manager," Luke Savoie's "Why We Debate: A Corporate Leadership Perspective," Amy Cram Helwich's "Leading Nonprofit Organizations," Lt. Col. Dave Haworth's "Off We Go," Marshall McMullen's "Engineering Discourse," and Matt Stannard's "Debate as Theater of Social Change."

The next section is devoted to exploring how the activity interacts with students outside the dominant cultural power structures. Both audience-centered debate and progressive forms of debate have been dominated by the white, male power structure. As such, the activity has rewarded the presentation styles of white males, academic research deemed appropriate by mainstream academia, and interrogated topics relevant to those in power. Thus, the activity has often ignored the academic contributions of those outside that structure. At times, it has actively excluded alternative viewpoints, alternative presentation styles, and those perceived to be the *other*. In the last two decades, we have seen an increasing number of individuals who are Black, Indigenous, and People of Color (BIPOC), who identify as lesbian, gay, bisexual, transgender, queer, intersex, asexual (LGBTQIA), and women push back against the expected paradigm. They challenge the narratives crafted by academic debate, our educational system, and society.

At this point in the text, I briefly take a step back from the world of competitive debate, to speak broadly about the challenges facing educators and their role in the classroom. In "Classrooms of Compassion," I highlight some of the realities we face in classrooms that are increasingly diverse. We do not educate students who enter the classroom with a monolithic American identity. Rather, our students come from diverse cultures, with different lived experiences that are shaped by race, religion, ethnicity, sexuality, and gender, not to mention socioeconomics and geography. Those experiences shape how students view (and interact with) the world, and it is our responsibility to build communities that welcome diversity in thought, experience, and communication.

In section 4, we explore nontraditional approaches to debate, commonly referred to as performance-based approaches. This paradigm approaches the activity from outside the "accepted" and "conventional" forms of communication rewarded within the debate community and mainstream education. Almost exclusively the purview of "minority" competitors, these students challenge our accepted notions of communication and rules. They communicate using culturally relevant methods and criticize the norms, conventions, and rules of the activity that stifle inclusivity.

Nicole D. Nave introduces the perspective of nontraditional approaches to debate through her chapter, "The Constant Pursuit of Inclusivity." She examines the historical roots of "performance-based" approaches, then discusses their importance in academia, the response from the traditional and progressive camps, and the relevance of the approach in students' lives.

Next, professor of education, Paul Ongtooguk and his daughter Pulgeenok Methanie Ongtooguk offer a glimpse into the importance of storytelling as an educational tool in "Living Inupiat Storytelling in Four Generations of Family." As the only nondebaters in this work, they use stories and examples of story to show how their culture shares meaning, history, and community through intentional storytelling outside the norms of Western educational and historical standards.

Their insights are followed by Jamal Burns's "Defining Black Cards," in which he uses his personal journey from traditional debating to performance debate to see how traditional approaches are insufficient for capturing the experiences of all our students. Yet, he was able to use nontraditional approaches to the activity to explore truth, while simultaneously becoming an activist within the debate community.

To illustrate what nontraditional debate looks like in practice, we turn to Desiree Hill and Maya McGregory's "Ship of Faith." In high school and college, they used poetry, rap, and dance as the channel to communicate their ideas in competitive debate rounds. Here, they translated one of their actual cases onto the written page. Their reflections and stage directions offer the reader insight into what nontraditional debate can look like in practice.

From these personal stories in debate, we turn to more practical applications beyond the academic world. Ravi Rao explores how debaters who embrace nontraditional approaches gain a unique ability to reap advantage in the workforce. He uses his experience as an employment coach to draw lessons from debate to career in "A Tool for Career Readiness."

Section 5, Power in Our Voices, serves as a capstone to the argument(s) of the text. It reinforces the ideas at the core of the book about academic, competitive debate. It begins with "In It Together," by Nicole Wanzer-Serrano, reflecting upon and reinforcing many of the themes presented in the text regarding the power of debate.

Rashad Howard's, "The Debater" closes the section and the book. I originally slated Rashad's chapter for the section on progressive, contemporary debating practices based on our shared time on the Air Force Academy debate team. When I received his chapter, however, I realized his story transcended any singular stylistic approach to debate. His deeply personal story also squarely centers the discourse within the educational and societal institutions that make debate—now more than ever—critical in our society.

Finally, I wish I could thank everyone who has been a vital part of my life, education, and career. Sadly (or *wonderfully*), there are too many who deserve recognition to mention them all. My parents for getting me into speech and debate. Teachers who helped shape me. ("Classrooms of Compassion" was heavily influenced by OU professors Eric Kramer and Aondover Tarhule—specific quotes and stories were cut during editing.) Coaches in Florida, Alaska, Missouri, and Arizona for amazing fellowship. Teammates and students who impacted my life in immeasurable ways. Becky for unimaginable support. Debaters I judged who frequently taught me. Paul for sharing the writers' journey . . . *finish your next book*. Steve and Luke for relentlessly promoting debate. Steve, thank you for the countless hours spent discussing the meaning of debate. Coaches and league directors/ staff who support their students for little compensation. Judges who make tournaments happen. SIU Press for working with me on not one, but two texts—especially Kristine Priddy, Jennifer Egan, Sarah Jilek, Linda Jorgensen Buhman, and Khara Lukancic. Not an exhaustive list, but many have contributed to my sanity over the last few years in ways they don't even know: Brett, Chad, Matt, Paul, Kameron, Sara, Tara, Nick, and more. Finally, to the contributors who shared their personal journeys, you are amazing!

Prologue: The Moment that Changed My Life

Shawn F. Briscoe

Friendship . . . is a virtue . . . For no one would choose
to live without friends even if he had all the other goods
. . . for 'when two go together,' they are more capable of
understanding and acting.

Aristotle, *Nicomachean Ethics*

Some moments have a profound effect on us, changing the course of direction or shaping our lives in remarkable ways. Sometimes we can pinpoint those exact moments. Often, however, they are fleeting and unrecognizable despite the mark they leave on us. I remember *the* moment—or more accurately a series of moments—that defined much of my life as it is today. Upon graduation from high school, I attended the United States Air Force Academy and served as an officer for six years. At that point, I left active duty to become an educator . . . to become a debate coach. And it all began in a moment of frustration and disappointment, just weeks before starting my freshman year at Nevada High School in rural Missouri.

I grew up knowing I wanted to be a pilot in the United States Air Force and eventually become an astronaut. I had that dream since kindergarten when I watched Luke Skywalker climb into the cockpit of his x-wing starfighter and wield a lightsaber. The dream grew in second grade when I learned about NASA and real-life astronauts. I held on to that dream throughout high school and my first two years in college. My life was mapped out. In the meantime, I loved the theatre. I participated in plays through middle school, church, and my hometown's Community Council on the Performing Arts. I desperately wanted to be a part of my high school's drama and theatre programs. However, life had something different in store for me.

I entered Nevada High School at the tail end of the Tim Gore-Ed Grooms-Debra Holman (Workman) era. These teachers had grown the speech, debate, drama, and theatre program to such success that freshmen were not allowed to simply join. At its height, the program drew more than a hundred people into its ranks. No small feat for a school barely topping seven hundred students. As a result, freshmen had to be invited into the fold . . . invited to participate in one aspect of the program. I remember the day clearly. School started in just a few weeks. The sun shone in a brilliant blue sky. The mail arrived. There was a letter for me. The return address said Nevada High School Forensics. Speech, Debate, and Theatre. I was ecstatic. I could barely contain the excitement as I tore into the envelope. The first line was something like: "Congratulations! Your eighth grade teachers have recommended you to us, and we have decided to invite you to be a debater at Nevada High School."

I was crushed. I tossed the letter on the table and sulked.

That night, my parents asked me about it. When I told them I was not joining the team, they could not believe I intended to walk away from such a successful program. I said something about wanting to participate in drama . . . to act. No way was I going to debate; that sounded *boring*. My dad asked if I had read the whole letter, which stated that I could switch to drama and theatre at the end of the year. He told me it was something I needed to do, and I grudgingly said okay.

Against my desires, I joined a storied program that made a mark not just in Missouri but on the national stage. When I joined the team, we heard about those who had led the team, dazzled people with their talent, and dominated on stage and in competition. Names like Russell Johnston, Lori

Barnes, Sarah Buchanan, Paul Hood, Laura Brewer, Jeff Krall, and the *Sree* brothers were spoken of with awe by the varsity members of the program.

Tim Gore—or Teeg, as we called him—introduced me to the world of academic, competitive debate. In hindsight, he was one of the top coaches in the nation. He taught us how to think, how to express ourselves, how to be gracious, how to be curious, how to be confident . . . and most of all, to question.

Yet, I went to my first tournament at a complete and utter loss. *Debate lets you know how little you really know.* I had excellent grades; I was near the top of my class; my teachers always recommended me for special activities and events; I was never afraid to voice my thoughts. So, I went to my first tournament with high expectations. The debate round started, and I seemed to have forgotten everything Teeg had taught us. I not only failed to speak my mind, I apparently forgot how to speak. I stumbled and stammered my way through an exceedingly short speech. I was not alone. The other team struggled, and my debate partner—Angie Wiltz—also seemed confused. A debate round that should have taken roughly an hour and a half, lasted less than twenty minutes. I was embarrassed. I wondered if people made a mistake thinking there was a place for me in this activity.

That's how it is with speech and debate. You are always at risk of encountering something that is beyond what you know or beyond what you are capable of accomplishing. We constantly read, studied, discussed, and practiced. We were regularly exposed to ideas, concepts, and patterns of thought that were new to us. Those experiences stretched us in ways we never imagined or even realized at the time. Those moments of feeling lost made the moments of competitive success all the sweeter.

In fact, *success in speech and debate could be every bit as intoxicating as in sports.* As a distance runner and soccer player, I knew the feelings associated with running a great race or playing in a tough game. It amazed me those same emotions could arise in an academic setting. In some ways, the thrill was more intense. Even as a spectator, I remember being exhilarated watching the likes of Josh Benner, Dawn Chapman, Chad Mathis, Jess Collins, and Sreedevi Sreenarasimhaiah in action. We all experienced these highs to more or lesser degrees during our time on the team. I remember my sixth tournament very well.

For the second time that season, my partner was not able to make the trip and I was debating in the novice division with Sarah Garwood—my superior in every way. The first time we debated together, I looked to Sarah to tell me what to do. At the second tournament, she agreed—at the urging of Teeg—to let me do my own thing. She was more talented than I, but this time I had to stand on my own two feet. We worked our way through the preliminary rounds undefeated, going 4–0. I was thrilled to find that we won the coin toss in quarterfinals and semifinals, so we could choose to defend the affirmative side of the topic. Speaking from a place of comfort and confidence, we won both rounds.

Then, things spiraled for me emotionally. We lost the coin toss in finals, and our opponents chose to go affirmative. Making things worse, it seemed everyone wanted to watch that championship round. A classroom that usually held around thirty students was packed with people sitting on the floor and along the windowsill. I still struggled to feel I deserved to be in debate, feel that I deserved to be paired with Sarah, and argue on the negative side of the topic. In short, I was a nervous wreck. I stood up for my second speech—a four-minute rebuttal. I was foundering through the first thirty to forty-five seconds when I made eye contact with one of our varsity standouts: Chad Mathis. He looked at me, cocked his head slightly to his right, squinted his eyes, grabbed his chin, and nodded as I spoke. At that moment, I was powerful. I was the best debater anyone had ever seen.

In truth, I have no idea whether I said anything intelligent in that round, but it did not matter. I was on top of the world, and I had a first-place trophy to show for our efforts.

Over the years, I accumulated many trophies. Nevada High School's speech and debate program was a powerhouse in the region. During the Gore-Grooms-Holman era, Nevada was a dominating force in the southwest corner of the state, winning multiple individual and team district championships. The squad brought home numerous awards from the Missouri State High School Activities Association state championship and qualified scores of students to the national championship tournament. In fact, Chad Mathis and Jess Collins placed among the top policy debate teams in the country at the end of their career. We knew how to win, and we had a *very large*, *very full* trophy case to show for it. While wins and losses, ranks, trophies, team sweepstakes, championships, and dreams of nationals dominated our thoughts in high school, those are not the things that dominate my memories of our team more than twenty-five years later.

Speech and debate was a community. We spent countless hours watching each other practice in class, after school, on the bus, in hotel rooms, in the

hallways of distant schools, and in competition itself. A typical Friday involved loading the bus for a long ride to Kansas City, Joplin, or Springfield.
Bus rides involved practice, preparation, jokes, stories, and blaring music.
Often, we spent the night at a Howard Johnson's in Springfield. We would
check in shortly after lunch—you could almost guarantee the *Princess Bride*
would be on TV as we geared up in our suits. We competed all afternoon and
evening. After a late-night dinner at Shoney's, we returned to the hotel room,
and then boarded the bus again sometime before dawn. In between rounds
of debate, speech, or interpretation of literature we talked with friends or
played a game of Spades.

Driving home, the bus would stop at some distant truck stop so the
coaches could call KNEM/KNMO so that an announcement could be made
on the hometown radio stations that we would return to Nevada High
School in less than an hour. In the days before cell phones, this was the
most convenient way to notify families that we would soon need rides. Upon
returning home late on Saturday night, a large group often descended upon
the bowling alley.

At competition, I have fond memories of watching my teammates perform and socializing with our friends from around the state. At home, there
were countless gatherings at Forensics Frolics. Families—like those of Mary
Beth Cunningham or Sarah Copeland—would open their homes for a Friday
evening that involved a potluck, a movie, games, or a disgusting display of
basketball ineptitude. (*Okay, that last one was just me.*)

Some of us even had the opportunity to travel out of state. My junior
year, Mr. Gore loaded a fifteen-passenger van and drove us to a large tournament in Chesterton, Indiana. Willie Denning sat in the front passenger
seat, and he played the cassette tape of the Steve Miller Band's *Live* album
on auto repeat all the way there and back. To this day, I cannot hear those
songs without thinking of the people on the team and speech and debate
tournaments.

As important as providing a sense of community, *the speech and debate
program taught us how to see another person's perspective, the value of seeing
that perspective, and empathy.* In speech, we scoured articles from sources
as varied as the *National Review, Christian Science Monitor*, the *New York
Times*, and the *Washington Post*. Simply, we needed to be familiar with
and understand any number of hot button topics to prepare our speeches.
Contestants in drama explored various pieces of literature, which exposed
them to characters with diverse backgrounds. When we watched them in

competition, we saw their interpretation of the literature come alive, making us feel the emotions of people presented with any number of conflicts. In theatre, we had to grasp the fictionalized reality of any number of characters to make our own performances ring true with the audience. In debate, we necessarily had to understand multiple sides of contentious topics. On the one hand, we had to understand the other point of view to build a convincing case for our own position or launch an effective attack upon our opponent's arguments. On the other hand, debate required us to switch sides, alternating between the affirmative and negative—pro and con. As a result, we had to see the world through the eyes of people who disagreed with us.

I spent roughly half my freshman year arguing against the United States federal government's space program. As someone who spent a lifetime dreaming of being an astronaut, this was challenging. Sometimes, the lessons were more difficult, but even more insightful. During my senior year, I entered a debate round where I was thrust into the position of arguing against my own political and social beliefs on a particularly contentious topic. As usual, it was challenging, but enlightening to argue against my personal convictions.

I learned another lesson after the round. As soon as the debate concluded, the judge yelled at us for being horrible human beings. That day, I realized you never know the circumstances that bring another person to their conclusions. She had no way of knowing my personal beliefs but reacted based on her assumptions about me as a human being. This is often the case for us in life. We may confront any number of people whose expressions, actions, or ideas upset us. In those instances, we must take the time to understand where they are coming from and what led them to that moment. We do not know what it is like to walk in another person's shoes. We do not know what circumstances led them to where they are at that moment. Perhaps we should reserve judgment until we take the time to have a meaningful conversation with them. In my case, I was unfairly attacked for something as trivial as a speech in a competitive debate environment. Imagine if someone was harassed for something more personal.

Ultimately, this program taught me there is extraordinarily little in the world that is black and white, absolute good and evil, completely right and wrong. Usually, there is a middle ground where the truth resides. Often, both perspectives are true. With time, energy, and effort, we can combine the truth found in multiple perspectives to create a world in which both sides are accepted and valued.

The speech and debate program also taught us critical skills. It taught us how to research, how to analyze, how to think creatively and critically, how to write, how to be efficient, and how to work with others to achieve something as a group. Nearly every day, we researched, explored ideas, wrote cases, crafted arguments, and developed characters. In competition, we tested our ideas against those of our opponents to persuade, convince, or entertain a judge. The educational benefits of participating in the activity are numerous.

We also learned a lot from planning and running the annual Nevada Forensic Festival. During my time in the program, our tournament was one of the largest in the state, drawing competitors from Kansas City, Springfield, Saint Louis, and many rural communities not to mention the occasional out-of-state teams. We had so many schools competing in the tournament that we often used four (of our town's six) different schools and a local church to accommodate the number of students entered in the tournament. It took countless hours working as a team to organize this event.

To say we were busy would be an understatement. We did everything, from recruiting hundreds of judges and timekeepers, scheduling the use of facilities, coordinating with teams from across the state, ordering trophies, planning meals, running topic draw for extemporaneous speaking, scheduling pairings, and tabulating the tournament. Even for those who did not become coaches, running our tournament still taught us countless lessons about organizing events in our personal and professional lives.

Participation in the program also inspired us to stretch ourselves in new ways. For some, it may have been watching a particularly emotional portrayal of a character in a school play. For others, it was seeing what one of our friends could do and deciding that we wanted to do that as well. For some, it may have been learning about a new idea or a challenging issue that led us to study more or take an active role in the community.

There was one moment during my junior year that opened my eyes to what debate at the highest levels looked like. I heard stories about the high school's national circuit. Despite hearing them, I did not truly grasp what it looked (*or sounded*) like. We were at a tournament in Springfield, Missouri, when we were assigned a debate round against some friends from Rockhurst High School, Eddie Bull and Eric Slusher. That team spent their summers at expensive debate camps and spent the year alternating between regional tournaments in Missouri and competing on the national circuit. It just so happened, that our judge for this round was a college debater at Missouri Southern State College (now Missouri Southern State University) named

Ken DeLaughder. Our opponents stood up and ran incredibly in-depth arguments while speaking at a rate that seemed incomprehensible.

My reaction was like that of Neo watching Morpheus jump from one skyscraper to another inside *The Matrix*, "Whoa." I was shocked and in awe. It inspired me to double-down on the activity and pursue it in college. Again, my participation was changing my life without my really knowing it.

Finally, *being a member of the theatre and speech and debate programs developed a sense of teamwork.* We worked together for the betterment of the team. We watched our peers perform their interpretations of literature and offered criticism. We conducted research on current events that we shared with teammates. We organized debate briefs that went through the Risograph machine so everyone could benefit from our collective efforts. Champ—or Varsity—competitors of the squad mentored the younger members of the team.

We celebrated each other's wins and consoled our friends in defeat. Many of us had the joy of working side-by-side with people with whom we had spent countless hours preparing for competition. For me, that moment culminated in the district tournament my senior year. It was a double elimination event. Lose twice, and you were out. If you lasted long enough, you got to move on to the National Forensic League (now the National Speech and Debate Association) National Championship. In my mind, the previous four years were building to this moment. Other than getting into the United States Air Force Academy, qualifying to nationals was the most important thing to me my senior year.

Robert Copple and I spent too many hours to count preparing for that tournament. In round one, we were assigned to debate the affirmative side of the resolution against Joplin [Missouri] High School's D team, meaning their coach deemed them the fourth best partnership on their squad. Joplin was our most serious rival that year, and they had the benefit of volunteer coaches who debated for Missouri Southern State College. Those college debaters even spent the final moments before the round helping them prepare to beat us. In the end, we won that round.

In round two, we were assigned the negative side of the topic against Neosho's top team. Unfortunately, we lost that round. That night, I ate dinner and returned to the hotel in a funk. We already had one loss. We now had to go undefeated throughout the remainder of the tournament. I figured that meant I was not going to qualify for nationals, and my high school debate career would end in disappointment.

Saturday morning, the pairings were released. We were going affirmative against Joplin C in round three. A couple of Missouri Southern debaters spent about thirty minutes preparing our opponents against our case. At the end of the round, we won.

Round four—another win while debating on the negative side of the topic.

In round five, we were assigned the affirmative against Joplin B. I was confident going into that round but started to get concerned as the Joplin D team, Joplin C team, and Missouri Southern debaters prepped our opponents against our case. After an hour and forty-five minutes, we won.

Round six, another win on the negative.

That brought us to the end of the tournament: round seven. If we won, we were district champions, and our ticket was punched to nationals. If we lost, my high school debate career was over. The pairings went up: Nevada A on the affirmative versus—Joplin A on the negative. For close to an hour, Missouri Southern debaters, Joplin B, Joplin C, and Joplin D prepped Joplin's top team against our case.

The round began with Robert's first affirmative constructive. The negative team gave a strong first speech, followed by one of my own. During the negative block—a thirteen-minute stretch of negative argumentation—I knew we were clearly losing that debate. They finally had our number, and the feelings of dread the evening before crept into my mind and my gut.

Robert stood up for a five-minute rebuttal speech, and we were clearly losing. As he spoke, I flipped my pen in the solemn knowledge that my career was ending. But then, roughly halfway through his speech I had a thought. I realized there was one way for us to win that debate. *If Robert would only say . . .* And, as the words ran through my mind, Robert spoke the words I was thinking verbatim. We knew each other so well; we were a hundred percent on the same page in that debate. I sat up straight, made eye contact with all three judges, and smiled. At that moment, I knew we would win. After the second speaker from the negative team gave her speech, I concluded the round in control, strategically well positioned, and persuasive.

And then we waited.

Robert and I looked at each other occasionally, glancing at our friends who filled the room, while the judges reviewed their notes.

The judges cast their ballots.

On a 3–0 decision, District Champions! We were headed to nationals!

To me, that was the pinnacle of speech and debate. Years later, I realized the program was far more important than a championship. I went on to debate at the Air Force Academy, advancing to elimination rounds at the collegiate national championship on two occasions and earning All-America honors my senior year. However, near the tail end of my sophomore year, I realized my time on the team at Nevada High School did more to prepare me for the rigors of the Air Force Academy than any class I took or activity/ club I participated in during high school. I began thinking about the importance of working with high school speech and debate students later in life.

Fast forward a few more years. As a first lieutenant in the United States Air Force, I began to realize my time on the Air Force Academy debate team did more to prepare me for a career in the military than anything else I did in college. I decided I would eventually alter my career path to become an educator. To become a speech and debate coach.

A moment that changed my life forever. Opening that letter during the summer before my freshman year had an unpredictable and profound impact on my life. I found: An activity that was life altering. A team of educators in Tim Gore, Ed Grooms, and Debra Holman that were caring, nurturing, inspiring, and brilliant. Friends, experiences, and memories that permeate my thoughts to this day. Perspectives instilled and skills developed that inspire and guide me in my daily life. I'm glad I was disappointed that summer. That invitation to join the debate team opened my eyes to a bigger world, and I wouldn't want it any other way.

Section One
The Nature of Competitive Debate

But the peculiar evil of silencing the expression of an opinion is, that it is robbing the human race . . . If the opinion is right, they are deprived of the opportunity of exchanging error for truth; if wrong, they lose, what is almost as great a benefit, the clearer perception and livelier impression of truth, produced by its collision with error.

John Stuart Mill, *On Liberty*

Debate has been described as esoteric and devoid of educational merit. It has been described as though it is on a collision course with itself, that the activity is imploding, and that it is destroying itself from the inside.

Those criticisms come from outsiders and even those within the debate community. Usually, they point to one or more of the stylistic approaches and say it is worthless and destroying the format. Often, students within the activity debate over the merits of the various stylistic approaches. These arguments often become heated, and even personal. Even when the arguments are civil, outsiders do not necessarily understand what is happening. Instead, they see an activity ripping itself apart.

The first section in this text explores the activity in its generalized form, irrespective of a particular stylistic approach. There are common elements in all three approaches that make debate a valuable and worthwhile activity.

1.
Debate and Disinformation

Sara B. Sanchez

As I watched coverage of former president Donald Trump's supporters breach the Capitol as Congress voted to certify the election on January 6, I found myself constantly reevaluating how I would approach this piece. I proposed a chapter on debate as a possible pathway out of a world of alternative facts, polarization, and declining civic engagement; however, as I watched the coverage, I was repeatedly struck by two things. The first was that there were people with debate experience on both sides (no pun intended) of the insurrection, so I needed to be able to unearth a reason that exposure to the same skills and training could lead to such wildly divergent positions. The second was a nagging suspicion that civic engagement was not nearly enough. After all, the insurrectionists were highly engaged, they were just dangerously wrong.

How does one reconcile an activity that produces both Matt Gaetz and Elizabeth Warren? That question bedeviled me for months while I tried to connect the dots between our current moment of democratic crisis and the possibility that debate may offer skills necessary to see us through to the other side. The problems that face our society run deep and it will likely take decades, constant effort, and substantial will from the populace to move the needle. But I am convinced that debate offers training in media literacy skills that are a necessary component of that effort. It may not be sufficient to ameliorate the broader crisis but disseminating those skills among the next generation of voters is a necessary step toward a solution.

I will look at three elements for this piece. First, I explain why I believe we find ourselves in such a fragile civic state. Second, I look at the approaches two former debaters take to politics and how they interact with the problems I identified. Finally, I evaluate the connections between the skill sets debate teaches best and the pressure points for changing our civic and political environment for the better. A note of caution, this is a lot more nuanced than a debate round and the timeline for fixing the massive problems we face collectively is long and arduous. But debate doesn't have to be a panacea to be a useful element of a necessary solution at a critical time.

In *How Democracies Die*, Steven Levitsky and Daniel Ziblatt explain the factors that contribute to democratic backsliding.[1] Specifically, they offer a prescient warning that modern democracies rarely succumb to a coup, they are much more inclined to erode as elected leaders deliberately weaken institutions. Ezra Klein summarized this succinctly for *Vox* in 2018:

> Demagogues and authoritarians do not destroy democracies. It's established political parties, and the choices they make when faced with demagogues and authoritarians, that decide whether democracies survive.[2]

To be clear, there are dozens of potential contributing factors that weaken democracies.[3] I want to focus on two I think debaters are particularly well trained to combat. The first is understanding the media environment that allows for blatantly false propaganda to take hold in the American electorate. The second is knowledge of how institutions work, their pressure points, and how to exact change.

One of the more maddening components of our current political environment is the way narratives morph over the course of time to suit preconceived political notions. House minority leader Kevin McCarthy went from begging Trump to call his supporters off as McCarthy and other congresspeople were under lockdown on January 6[4] to refusing to participate in an independent bipartisan commission to investigate that event.[5] It is illustrative of the type of narrative manipulation we see daily and easier to identify when one understands how to frame an argument while shifting that frame over time.

Perhaps no current congressman is better at shifting those frames by peddling sound bites, bluster, and obfuscation than Florida congressman and former debater, Matt Gaetz. Gaetz may have fallen out of favor with some in the Republican Party[6] as he's being investigated in connection to a sex trafficking case, but his own district would still vote to reelect him according to at least one poll from Victory Insights.[7] Amy Davidson Sorkin tracked the bizarre scandal and Matt Gaetz's rise in a Republican Party increasingly characterized more by outrage musical chairs than any coherent governing agenda.[8] The bottom line is Gaetz's supporters in his district do not believe anything negative they hear about him and are inclined to default to his public relations campaign, facts be damned. It turns out you can build a career as a mainstay on right wing media as long as you are good enough *owning the libs*.

Debate may train some to survive, and even thrive, with a public relations offensive aided and abetted by a polarized media environment that allows them to characterize all opposition as lies. However, debate also trains citizens to see through those tactics.

Another former debater, Senator Elizabeth Warren, ran for president under the slogan *she has a plan for that*. While ultimately unsuccessful at winning the White House, the apex of her campaign was a period where she explained dozens of policy plans to address America's biggest problems. She had a plan to increase childcare for working parents, another for alleviating student loan debt, and more. She spoke to crowds of thousands of supporters, never shying away from facts and nuance. Warren is a lawyer, and importantly, a former teacher. I found myself drawn to the way she took complex issues and explained them in ways anyone could understand. I was impressed she seemed committed to building a constituency that wanted change while understanding how difficult it could be to enact. I loved her commitment to fight for big, structural change.

I also appreciated that when she didn't ultimately win her party's nomination, Warren pushed on. As she documents in her book *Persist*, Warren picked herself up and kept fighting after seeing messages of support after ending her campaign.[9] More importantly, she kept working behind the scenes. As *Politico* reported in March, Warren's staffers and allies hold many prominent positions in President Joe Biden's administration dealing with finance policy:

The Warren recruits mark a victory for the progressive movement, which has supported her yearslong "personnel is policy" campaign to chip away at the dominance of corporate insiders in setting policy for Democrats. Those who took on the fight with Warren say they're pleasantly surprised it has produced so many results under Biden, reflecting a new emphasis on inequality and challenging corporate power. Industry lobbyists, in turn, warn that banks, private equity firms and consumer lenders should pay close attention.

The appointments "confirm that Sen. Warren will be the most influential voice in the financial policy debate under the new administration," said Karolina Arias, a former Democratic Senate aide who is now a partner at Federal Hall Policy Advisors.[10]

It does not end with economic policy. *Politico* goes on to acknowledge key appointments in the Education Department, the Department of Health and Human Services, and the National Security Council.

If you stay in debate long enough you participate in a lot of debates as a competitor, judge, and coach. As a result, you evaluate hundreds, maybe even thousands of arguments. A second-year debater could identify the difference between the sound bites, bluster, and obfuscation of a Gaetz argument and the meticulous research and expertise of an Elizabeth Warren policy proposal. One takes advantage of a polarized media environment to "win" on what is basically a pseudo-clever framework trick to nullify the opposition and solidify support. The other considers the roles and resources of the federal government and makes a case for how to best change that machinery to achieve a specific policy end. Only one of these strategies has a backup plan aimed at achieving meaningful change.

The crux of the problem we face as a society is that the number of people with the skills to make that comparison has dwindled, and it isn't necessarily their fault. Debate programs have been in decline for decades. Broader content focus shifted to STEM and knowledge of history and civics were hit hard. Educating for American Democracy estimates we spend five cents on civic engagement for every fifty dollars per student we spend on STEM education.[11] It is not difficult to see why skills like evaluating the strength of claims and warrants, recognizing bias in sources, and identifying logical fallacies in content areas that are more prone to subjectivity and disagreement like politics, civics, and history have atrophied as a result.

That disinvestment from civic education happened at precisely the moment people need those skills most. In 1972–73 as Watergate unfolded, there were three news networks and two papers of record chasing down the facts and causes of political rot in our culture. While they may have had slightly different timing on their news leaks, those organizations agreed on the core principles of the duties of a president, the role of the Department of Justice, and the threshold for removing an unfit individual from the Oval Office. Critically, they also agreed on uncovering a set of key facts that would determine what *unfit* meant and presenting them to the American people to evaluate in good faith.

Forty-eight years later, the three news networks compete with three main cable networks chasing twenty-four-hour news cycles. They, in turn, compete with upstart networks and YouTube channels designed to pull the fringe further to the left or right when there are disagreements. The papers of record have survived but many of the smaller and mid-sized newsrooms in cities and towns have not. And all of them must compete in an online environment where snazzy website design and cleverly phrased credentials allow the fulminations of interest groups to masquerade as news.[12]

That news environment would be dangerous enough for misinformation, but we do not just encounter news from our dozens of outlets of choice. We encounter news through the social media feeds of friends and family sharing misinformation unwittingly. While tech companies have promised improvements in how information is spread on their platforms to attempt to combat blatant misinformation[13] the most sensational stories often spread the quickest.[14] They are rarely disputed before they have reached thousands or even millions of potential voters. Even after tech companies increased their defenses against misinformation, it was revealed the vast majority of false claims related to the COVID-19 vaccine stemmed from just twelve people.[15] It requires constant vigilance to identify credible sources and question the claims made in misinformation. Without some basis in evaluating evidence and arguments most citizens do not have a chance.

Additionally, political conversation has gotten so contentious that many would prefer not to have it at all. They opt instead for phrases like *that's just your opinion* and *we'll agree to disagree* as if the facts that underlie one's conclusions do not impact the credibility of those opinions. The problems we face as a society are too dire to put off wrestling with them because it makes people uncomfortable. For all its flaws, successful debaters must listen to, evaluate, and come to terms with the other side's claims. Debate also leaves open the possibility that your favorite idea may not win the day. The other side may have a more compelling problem or solution. The humility to acknowledge that your side is not always right is in short supply in political conversation in contemporary America. It is easier to retreat to information bubbles that reaffirm what you already believe.

Debate is often the first place students begin to conceive of the value of picking a side of an issue and advocating for it with facts, as opposed to merely discussing it theoretically as if all sides could be true. It is the first place they are taught the value of listening to the other side's responses to that argument, grappling with them, and answering them to make their own advocacy better. Don't get me wrong, debate has a lot of flaws. It is also a place where asinine arguments can be victorious because of a sleight of hand. A place where students can occasionally be rewarded for bluster, rather than skill. Debate could be a training ground for misinformation in the wrong hands.

But the people best equipped to distinguish the charlatan from the leader are those trained with the knowledge of how their positions were crafted, supported, and presented. It is imperative that more citizens understand the logical building blocks of political statements and policy proposals. We are inundated with a stunning amount of information and disinformation daily. Having the ability to quickly fact-check material and sources is an essential life skill, and debate is one of the best activities at teaching it. Training the next generation to distinguish between facts and bluster is a necessary, albeit insufficient, component of restoring the health of our society and democracy.

Notes

1. Steven Levitsky and Daniel Ziblatt, *How Democracies Die* (New York: Penguin Random House Publishing, 2018).

2. Ezra Klein, "How Democracies Die, Explained: The Problems in American Democracy Run Far Deeper than Trump," *Vox*, February 2, 2018, accessed August 4, 2021, https://www.vox.com/policy-and-politics/2018/2/2/16929764/how-democracies-die-trump-book-levitsky-ziblatt.

3. Rising inequality as the result of growing economic gaps between the rich and poor, structural racism, and deliberate moves both by the courts and legislatures to weaken some people's access to the franchise and other challenges face democracy.

4. Jamie Gangel, Kevin Liptak, Michael Warren, and Marshall Cohen, "New Details about Trump-McCarthy Shouting Match Show Trump Refused

to Call Off the Rioters," *CNN*, February 12, 2021, accessed August 4, 2021, https://www.cnn.com/2021/02/12/politics/trump-mccarthy-shouting-match-details/index.html.

5. Chris Marquette, "McCarthy Has 'No' Regrets Opposing Jan. 6 Independent Commission: GOP Leader Opposes Select Committee As Well," *Roll Call*, June 25, 2021, accessed August 4, 2021, "https://www.rollcall.com/2021/06/25/mccarthy-has-no-regrets-opposing-jan-6-independent-commission/.

6. Jeremy Herb, Ryan Nobles, and Dana Bash, "Republicans Keep Their Distance from Matt Gaetz," *CNN*, April 6, 2021, accessed August 4, 2021, https://www.cnn.com/2021/04/06/politics/matt-gaetz-republican-reaction-congress/index.html.

7. Jacob Ogles, "Poll Finds Majority of GOP Voters in Matt Gaetz's District Still Stand with Him," *Florida Politics*, April 11, 2021, accessed August 4, 2021, https://floridapolitics.com/archives/419120-poll-finds-majority-of-republicans-in-matt-gaetzs-home-district-stand-with-him/.

8. Amy Davidson Sorkin, "The G.O.P.'s Matt Gaetz Problem," *New Yorker*, April 11, 2021, accessed August 4, 2021, https://www.newyorker.com/magazine/2021/04/19/the-gops-matt-gaetz-problem.

9. Elizabeth Warren, *Persist* (New York: Metropolitan Books 2021).

10. Zachary Warmbrodt, "'Most Influential Voice': Warren's Network Spreads throughout Biden Administration," *Politico*, March 15, 2021, accessed August 4, 2021, https://www.politico.com/news/2021/03/15/elizabeth-warren-aides-biden-administration-475653.

11. "Our Vision," About Us, Educating for American Democracy, 2021, accessed August 4, 2021, https://www.educatingforamericandemocracy.org/our-vision/. Author's note: Educating for American Democracy is a diverse collaboration among over three hundred academics, historians, political scientists, K–12 educators, district and state administrators, civics providers, students, and others aimed at strengthening history and civic education in the United States

12. Chris Hayes and Davey Alba, "Your Local Disinformation," *Why Is This Happening?* Podcast audio, December 8, 2020, https://www.stitcher.com/show/why-is-this-happening-with-chris-hayes/episode/your-local-disinformation-with-davey-alba-200215015.

13. Nick Statt, "Major Tech Platforms Say They're 'Jointly Combating Fraud and Misinformation' about COVID-19," *The Verge*, March 16, 2020, accessed August 4, 2021, https://www.theverge.com/2020/3/16/21182726/coronavirus-covid-19-facebook-google-twitter-youtube-joint-effort-misinformation-fraud.

14. Peter Dizikes, "Study: On Twitter, False News Travels Faster than True Stories," *MIT News*, March 8, 2018, accessed August 4, 2021, https://news.mit.edu/2018/study-twitter-false-news-travels-faster-true-stories-0308.

15. Shannon Bond, "Just 12 People Are Behind Most Vaccine Hoaxes on Social Media, Research Shows," *NPR*, May 14, 2021, accessed August 4, 2021, https://www.npr.org/2021/05/13/996570855/disinformation-dozen-test-facebooks-twitters-ability-to-curb-vaccine-hoaxes.

2.
Truth, A Casualty of Intellectual Warfare?

Shawn F. Briscoe

What is the nature of competitive, academic debate? Who are the participants? Why are they there? The stage is set: four high school students prepare to do battle in front of hundreds of onlookers as they vie for the New Jersey state debate championship. The narrator for the 2007 film *Rocket Science* intones, "One team on the affirmative arguing for the resolution. The other on the negative, tearing it down . . . And so it goes. The high school debate, like the war that rips through your city and ravages everything in its path. The kids wielding words like weapons and brandishing ideas like axes. Nothing else mattered in that final round; there was no world beyond it."[1] If debate is a war, then who or what pays the price of battle? What is the collateral damage? Some contend that in the battle for championships and scholarships, the casualty is truth. Many become despondent in the priority placed upon the game, seemingly above all else. Despite its competitive nature and despite its flaws, scholastic debate is fundamentally still a pursuit that illuminates truth.

Truth.

As educators, most coaches hold passion for knowledge and the corresponding quest for truth in the highest regard. In *Nicomachean Ethics,*

Aristotle argued that as rational beings we should defend and pursue the truth at all times. As debaters and educators, his words connecting debate with truth should have significant meaning for us. After all, we grapple with the principles that guide us, controversial issues that challenge us, and political issues that divide us. Throughout the course of a year, we engage in dozens, if not hundreds, of academic debates over these very ideas.

Debate was once seen as a grand pursuit for truth. Today, it has been called into question. In the 2008 documentary *Debate Team*, 1969 National Debate Tournament finalist Michael Haller of the University of Houston stated, "Debate, on the other hand, is a search for truth. Or, at least it was. Now, I don't know what it is today."[2] His comment was preceded by a litany of debaters and coaches making statements like: the activity is "infinitely criticizing," "we do not necessarily look for the truthful thing to argue," and "debate isn't really about truth seeking."[3]

There are many in contemporary debating who contend that policy debate, in particular, is no longer about the truth—that it is simply a game that does little if anything to aid our ability to understand. To hit that point home, then-competitor Aaron Hardy explained in the same documentary that, "When I'm there, I'm there for a singular purpose and it's not to hang out with Tarloff at the bar. It's not to make friends. It's not to, you know, do anything other than win." To outsiders—and many within the debate community—it appears the activity is no longer an academic pursuit. It no longer helps us find the truth or better understand the world. Perhaps, worse still, it is a cutthroat endeavor where winning isn't everything, it is the *only* thing—relationships be damned. The only thing that matters is defeating the *other* who has been assigned to be one's opponent in that round of competition.

Although noteworthy, these indictments of debate view the activity through an inappropriate paradigm. When analyzed precisely, debate in all its permutations is still very much about promoting understanding and truth. To understand the activity, one must begin with reflecting on what people think debate is. Many hold an idealized version of smart, young people standing up in front of an audience and defending the notions of justice. Consider the fictionalized versions of Wiley College's debaters in the movie *The Great Debaters*. Denzel Washington, portraying Melvin B. Tolson, coaches his students to gallantly stand firm against racism and social injustice. These debaters are passionate, eloquent, and—most importantly—*always* on the right side of every argument. While the film is fantastic, it does a disservice for those wishing to understand the meaning of competitive debate and, in many ways, reinforces some misconceptions.

There are four common faulty assumptions people make when examining the merits—or lack thereof—of competitive debate. First, they believe something they do not understand must be devoid of academic value. They claim its esoteric nature makes it the purview of strange individuals who lack connection with the real world. Debate is a complex beast. The nature of argumentation takes years to explore. The jargon and speaking styles used by debaters as a form of shorthand among experts seem artificial, cryptic, and devoid of real-world application. In 2014, the *American Conservative* captured this perspective in an article titled "How to Speak Gibberish and Win a National Debate Title." In it, the author made such statements as, "This is a politically correct fraud," "We must privilege gibberish," "You will see an adult woman appear to be having a psychotic break as she addresses the audience," and "Competitive debate is a completely insane phenomenon."[4]

Furthermore, the issues students discuss are studied in semester-long undergraduate and graduate courses, and each debate may be comprised of three to seven of those issues. The students themselves come to the activity with different cultural, social, and economic backgrounds. Each student is informed by those backgrounds and approaches the activity, public speaking, and the issues from a unique place. Bring all of that together in a single environment and it appears people are moving in all different directions, speaking in gibberish, and in a language foreign to the observer. Take a step back to view the whole picture, and one realizes that students are grappling with complex ideas from different vantage points. Taken together, they collectively explore these complex ideas, helping all the participants better understand them.

Second, critics begin with the fundamental assumption that a single debate round illuminates the truth. This is where many of the quotes from the documentary mentioned earlier take root. It is incredibly rare for a single competitive debate round to lead to enlightenment. The debate rounds are too short for that to occur. Furthermore, the nature of competition means that debaters are vying for a coveted *win* from the judge. As a result, debates are generally focused on an argument that can be won, a mistake made by an opponent, an errant use of logic, a strategic or tactical gambit, and so forth. View debate from a larger context, however, and things are different. Debaters engage in countless hours of research on difficult topics. They spend just as many hours piecing together the foundations of arguments. They grapple with those ideas in competition. They are forced to debate both sides of those issues in alternating debate rounds. They receive feedback from judges after the debate. And every debater participates in dozens of, if not more than a hundred, debate rounds each year. If you take the long view, you see that debaters learn the intricacies of complex issues, find that the other side has valid points, develop empathy, and discover meaningful ways to navigate the social and political landscape.

Take one of my many experiences in collegiate debate. Being a man on the Air Force Academy debate team made me a great target for teams that wanted to run an argument rooted in feminism. Round after round, they charged that as men and as cogs in the patriarchy of the U.S. military, we were uniquely to blame for much of the harm in society. Round after round we listened to their argument, and we responded. Tournament after tournament we researched the foundations of patriarchy and the perspectives of various notions of feminism. We shared our thoughts with our teammates. We listened to the thoughts of our friends who attended different schools. And . . . we found ourselves changed human beings. Although no single debate round uncovered the truth in patriarchy *or* feminism, the process—the act of engagement—changed my perspectives. It altered my leadership style. Would I still go on to become an officer in a large, bureaucratic, vertically designed, power-projecting machine? Yes. However, upon graduation, I also led my airmen by seeking inclusion, consensus building, and shared decision-making as often as I could. I also made compassion the foundation of my leadership style and sought to understand the perspectives, wants, and needs of the people for whom I was responsible. Simply put, participating in debate exposes individuals to different ways of thinking, and that exposure leaves an impact upon the participants.

Third, many within the debate community confuse winning and competitive success with academic gains. Nothing could be further from the truth. Learning stems from grappling with the issues, not by earning a win from a judge. In a competitive setting, the best idea may not always win, but students learn how to analyze issues, construct coherent arguments, frame the issues so they are compelling to an audience, and present those ideas persuasively. One of my former high school students, David Williams, once explained to me that his study of arguments in debate led him to the conclusion that winning and losing could not adequately explain whether he was successful at a debate tournament. Rather:

he defined success as a round in which he improved upon his previous debates, could meaningfully self-critique his efforts, and learned something new. By contrast, he defined failure as a debate tournament in which he repeated previous mistakes, failed to identify his points of weakness, or floated through the tournament without being pushed to think in new and different ways. Thus, he could be a tournament champion and fail, or he could lose every round and be happy at the end of the day.[5]

In other words, we do not necessarily discover truth and meaning through winning and losing. It is the journey itself that produces change in the individual.

Finally, the critics of debate define truth with too narrow a lens. They hope to find a monumental *a-ha* moment at the conclusion of the debate, which can drive reform throughout society. As noted earlier, there are flaws with taking that singular view. Beyond that, there is also the truth of who we are as individuals and as a global society. The members of debate teams become close-knit families who lean on and can depend on one another. Student debaters serve as mentors and leaders for lesser experienced members of their squads. Debaters support their opponents from other teams and form ties, which last a lifetime. It is not by accident that many of the contributors to this work refer to the *debate community*. We truly begin to understand and value others.

Debate is an exceptionally fun activity for the participants. Because it is a competitive activity, debaters hope to win ballots and earn trophies. In that pursuit, do debaters choose the path that will win rather than the one that will help us to better understand the world? Conversely, do debaters learn a great deal about the world and each other? Yes, *and* yes. Both of those ideas can be true. They are not mutually exclusive notions. Debate is an incredibly impactful activity. It absolutely helps us understand the world and the people in it. It can bring us together as a closer community. Its lessons can and do help former debaters shape the world in beneficial ways.

Notes

1. *Rocket Science*, directed by Jeffrey Blitz (2007; B&W Films, Duly Noted, HBO Films, and Rocket Science Inc., 2007). DVD.

2. *Debate Team*, directed by B. Douglas Robbins (2008; Green Lamp Pictures in association with Long Strand Studios, 2008), DVD.

3. *Debate Team*.

4. Rod Dreher, "How to Speak Gibberish and Win a National Title," *American Conservative*, May 10, 2014, accessed September 1, 2020, https://www.theamericanconservative.com/dreher/how-to-speak-gibberish-win-a-national-debate-title/.

5. Shawn F. Briscoe, "Forensics: A Socio-Emotional Learning Space," *Rostrum* 83, no. 4 (December 2008): 58.

3.
Finding Home

Alex Berry

One of the most important and well-known collegiate debate rounds, the championship round of the 2013 National Debate Tournament, featured an affirmative team that argued about the importance of making debate a home. Debate is a highly competitive activity. It can be exclusionary and is far from free of oppression and marginalization. Thinking of debate as a home was—and is—nothing short of transformative and revolutionary. In 2013, a team of Black queer debaters—while arguing for a national championship—challenged us to imagine debate as a home.

The idea of home has always been important to me. I looked for home in many places: a church youth group, different summer camps, and so many people. I bounced around, looking for a place to call my own, looking for a place to belong, looking for a place to fit. No "home" ever lasted.

Debate changed that.

I cannot pinpoint exactly what drew me to debate or compelled me to stay, but almost as soon as I joined the squad, I knew I had found something special. I felt a sense of belonging that has only grown over the years. Debate gave me an identity, a community, a passion. Debate is the feeling of getting to your house after a long day, taking your pants off, and getting into bed. It is the feeling of watching the Saint Louis Blues win the Stanley Cup for the first time ever and everyone around you is jumping around and losing their minds and shout-singing the Blues anthem for the season, Laura Branigan's "Gloria." It is seeing your friend after a long time apart and hugging them so tightly neither one of you can breathe. It is spending all night working on a difficult problem and the elation of finally reaching the solution. It is laughing so hard your stomach hurts, and it is crying so hard your eyes hurt. It is pure joy, desperation, agony, hope, loss, exhaustion, laughter, frustration, excitement, love. It is home.

That sounds silly, and I get it. It is *just* an after-school activity. How could it possibly be that important? Honestly, I do not know. At face value, it does not really make sense. But I do know that it is the most challenging, most rewarding, and most fun thing I have ever done. It is also where I built some of my most important relationships.

I do not remember how many tournaments I won my senior year. I could not tell you a win-loss record or what speaker awards I won. I know I had competitive success, but that is about it. I could tell you a little about specific debate rounds, but mostly I could tell you about funky or creative arguments people read, funny moments, or particularly interesting advocacies. Winning was fun and losing sucked, but years later that is not what I remember, and that is probably because of my team's culture.

Before every round, my coach would tell us "Good luck, have fun, learn things"; and her first questions after a round ended were always if we had fun and if we learned something. It is because of that, that my memories of high school debate involve eating delicious doughnuts with my team on day three of the National Speech and Debate Association's (NSDA) national qualifying tournament, blasting Taylor Swift in the car on the way to the Clayton High School tournament my junior year, one of my teammates doing a freestyle rap to hype me up before the championship round of a Saint Louis Urban Debate League tournament, laughing with my partner during practice, breaking the one clap rule[1] to cheer for my friends, and preparing for the culminating tournament at summer debate camp with my friends on the Fourth of July while listening to "Mr. Brightside" and eating cream cheese bacon pizza from the best pizza place in Lawrence, Kansas. For the life of me, I cannot remember the exact wording of the domestic surveillance debate topic, but I can still tell you my coaches' Starbucks orders (*Nitro cold brew with sweet cream for Laura and a hot Pike Place roast with a couple raw sugars for Shawn).* Those small moments and inside jokes are infinitely more important and memorable to me than winning, and I think that is true of most debaters. Although . . . maybe it is weird that I also have fond memories of late nights spent highlighting my evidence, skipping class to time how long it took to read prewritten arguments, and annotating research while getting a pedicure before my senior pictures. Debate is a competitive activity, but it is also so much more.

We often talk about community, community-building, and the debate community, and it is even contested whether a *debate community* actually exists, but the relationships we build are undeniable, important, and unique. Students, coaches, and judges build relationships full of mutual support, understanding, and encouragement (and sometimes disagreement and animosity). Debate, especially at the national circuit level, is such a small world—it seems like everyone knows everyone else. People across the country connect with each other through this weird and wonderful activity.

Of course, debate is not perfect—far from it. Some students face racial microaggressions, toxicity, and gender-based and sexual violence. We cannot ignore that part of the story as it does a disservice to survivors. The people in the activity can be its best and its worst aspect at once. Holding both of those facts simultaneously is tricky.

It is difficult to reconcile that the community and activity I love have also caused physical and emotional harm to me and others. Knowing how beautiful and important debate can be, though, serves as a catalyst and inspiration for change. There is a great deal of work to be done, and many have committed to doing it. We owe it to each other and our students to continue the work.

Ultimately, I met some of my closest friends through my team, debate tournaments, and debate camps. Some of my most important role models and mentors are people I met through debate. These people are truly my family and the support I received from them has been life changing. My coaches and debate partner were some of the first people I came out to as transgender. Coming out was terrifying and a long process. In many ways, the unconditional support and love from my community made that possible. My friends and teammates respected my personal timeline in coming out and were always respectful, affirming, and supportive. It was with their encouragement and compassion that I found the strength to come out to my parents and begin testosterone hormone replacement therapy. I truly believe the people I met through debate—many of whom are queer and trans—have made my transition possible.

Two full years after attending debate camp in high school, I took a trip to Kansas to visit friends with whom I have maintained strong relationships over the years. I have a *million* stories about the people I met through debate and the ways they impacted my life. It is such a small world, and the best example of that is probably a policy debate round at the National Catholic Forensic League's Grand National Tournament in May of 2019. A team from Kansas, friends of friends that I had helped with research, were debating a team from Saint Louis that I did not know but wrote an argument for as a favor to their coach (who was also a college friend of my own coach), and they were judged by a friend of mine from Tulane and another dear friend's former teammate.

One of the most important sites of community-building in debate is debate camp. This is another one of those things that sounds strange to people not involved with the activity (*and may be one of the reasons my parents think debate is a cult*), but debate camp was always the highlight of my summer. I loved immersing myself in my favorite thing with people who were equally passionate, and debate camp was instrumental in my growth as a debater. More than that, though, it is where I built some incredibly important and lasting relationships. In just four weeks over two summers at the Jayhawk Debate Institute (JDI) at the University of Kansas, I met some of my best friends.

Community at the JDI looked like going on Pokémon Go raids as a lab, watching *Moana*, and playing a fifteen-person game of Down by the Banks when we should have been doing a speaking drill. It was little silly moments of laughter and connection, but it was also very intentionally fostered by lab leaders and camp staff. A couple days into camp, after one of my lab leaders overheard me admit to a friend that I had been anxious about going to the dining hall because I didn't know anyone, he instituted a family meal policy—the entire lab had to eat lunch together every day. My other lab leader wrestled a 5-hour ENERGY away from me during the camp tournament because she was concerned about my caffeine consumption. I had friends who accepted me and adult role models who cared about me as both a debater and a person. Camp was incredibly special for me, and I think that is true for many debaters. Time and time again, I see my friends and colleagues care for their labbies the way mine cared for me. A friend of mine bought cold medicine for one of their students (and then a different type of cold medicine because he could not take pills). My friends will regularly buy food for their students, even when they are unwilling to spend money on themselves.

Even in college I found my home in debate. I felt lost during my first semester at Tulane—hundreds of miles from my parents, lonely, and struggling academically. Several weeks into the semester, the Tulane Parliamentary Debate Team hosted an information session. With team leaders and the other wide-eyed freshmen in that conference room, I began to tear up. Afterward, I asked one of the presenters for a hug—I finally felt like I had come home.

Debate is competitive, but there are beautiful moments of connection and care. This is true even at tournaments, the literal epitome of competition. I am from the Eastern Missouri NSDA district, and I am pretty sure it is the best district in the country because of the way we care for each other. My favorite thing about Eastern Missouri is the way we came together in June of 2018. On June 15, days before the NSDA national tournament, an Eastern Missouri debater died. His name was Haran Kumar. He was funny and smart as hell. He was taking a gap year to do some coding thing, and then he was going to Harvard where he told a friend he would get him Malia Obama's autograph. Our senior year, a self-declared "Confederate" ran for a school board position and Haran started a campaign to make sure she did not win. He made signs and organized protests on both social media and at physical locations. She ended up with a laughably small percentage of the vote, in part because of his dedication to people.

On June 17, we left for the NSDA National Championship Tournament. I cried three times with my coach on the airplane to Fort Lauderdale. Haran should have been there. The whole week, every single East MO debater wore a blue and white ribbon—his school's colors—pinned on our suit jackets and blouses. *He would have hated it.*

Haran disliked stuff like that. He hated awards ceremonies. He thought they were stupid and superficial. Pieces of plastic didn't mean anything. He would never compromise his beliefs for a win (but he almost always won). He thought education, friendships, and experiences were infinitely more valuable than a shiny piece of plastic. He always made award ceremonies into a joke. One time, he stood on stage eating from a bag of peanuts. Another time, he wore a suit jacket over a sweatshirt and put a tie on his head. He was goofy and silly—and he would have hated the ribbons. Haran changed the way I think about debate, and when my students or teammates are discouraged about a loss, I tell them about Haran. He would be happy even if he lost every debate round, as long as he learned something and had fun. As fun as it is to win trophies, they melt in the microwave.

His high school, Parkway West, hosts the first tournament of the season in Eastern Missouri. In the fall of 2018, the team t-shirts featured a longhorn—the school mascot—with green hair, just like Haran's, and the back of the shirts featured a joke he often made. They did not give awards for the tournament, either. Awards are expensive, and students brought in toys, shoes, games, and stuffed animals. Those were the trophies. They donated the money they would have spent on trophies to Every Child's Hope, an organization in Saint Louis that provided therapy to Haran. Several days before he died, he told his mom that he wished he could give them millions of dollars. Parkway West ended up donating almost $800 from that tournament, and if you look on Instagram, you will find a couple posts tagged #TrophiesMeltIntheMicrowave.

That is what debate is to me. It's not wins or losses. It is laughter and friendship and community and love. When I first taught at a debate camp in 2019, my middle school novices begged me to lead a junior varsity lab the next summer so I could teach them again. When I was a resident advisor in the dorms at the Women's Debate Institute, several of the students told me I have "big sibling energy." The connections I made through debate are life-changing, life-sustaining, and lifelong.

Those relationships are why I know debate will always be a part of my life. Even in high school, I knew I wanted to stay involved in debate because I couldn't imagine my life without it, but hearing my kids call me "Mom" solidified it for me. Debate can be so ugly and messy and imperfect, but it is also so beautiful and special in a million different ways. I have been lucky to find my home and family in debate, and I know that I am home to stay.

Notes
1. Many tournaments, to speed up the awards ceremony, request audience members only offer a single clap for individuals receiving awards.

4.
Putting Debate Skills to Work

Aubrey Semple

The outbreak of COVID-19 upended society in numerous ways. The effect on the economy and by extension people's livelihoods has been especially severe. Simply, the current job market is particularly challenging. As the United States's economy is changing more and more by the day, crucial questions continue to hold relevance. How can someone stand out as an ideal job candidate in the job hunt? How can someone stand out in front of potential employees in an environment where millions are applying for unemployment daily? How can someone leverage their experiences to better situate themselves within the job market?

These questions highlight the anxiety that many face within our debate community. One harsh reality is that we must face the cruel truth that no one is immune to being unemployed. Unemployment sits dormant in the reality of some and to be able to climb out of that requires us to remember, as debaters, we develop uniquely portable skills that make us future assets to organizations or companies. Having the fortune of being a debate coach, former entrepreneur, and a former administrator of an education nonprofit in one of the largest cities in the United States, there are tricks that I have learned from debate that can be applied as strategies to make you stand out among other job applicants. As a debater, judge, coach, and administrator of a league, I have also experienced the full spectrum of performative approaches to debate. I can say with certainty, all of them prepare students for the job market.

This chapter explores the tips and tricks debaters have in our arsenal to make us stand out as exceptional candidates for that future job, in a market with scarce employment opportunities yet full of talented people. Even as we recover from the economic implications of COVID-19, we must remember that the job market will always be competitive. We must consider how to exploit our specialized talent of research, oral communication, and critical thinking skills to get that job.

What You Know versus What You Can Prove

Succeeding in the job hunt starts with your defense of what makes you valuable to your potential employer. Today, they want to have a sense of what intrinsic value you can provide to their company or organization. Think about how your ability to construct and defend an idea makes you a valuable asset to them. These employers seek employees that can use their skills to help elevate the companies' vision, which ultimately helps their bottom line. While the resume and qualifications begin to create that picture, there are many things individuals bring to the table. Furthermore, it is rare for applicants to exist in a vacuum. Typically, there are several if not dozens of qualified applicants. As such, the most likely new hire is the one who sets themselves apart from the field by demonstrating how they will uniquely benefit the employer in ways that other applicants will not.

Like competitive debate, we can use various strategies to stand out as an ideal candidate for employment. In any given debate, competitors use tools such as a *round overview* to paint a picture of why your position is more favorable than their opponent's. In the overview, the speaker isolates a scenario where there is an issue that justifies an action to occur. Consequently, the speaker then reveals why their action, such as the advocacy of one's position is preferable to the opponent's advocacy. In the competitive job market, winning the job sometimes comes down to how you paint a picture as to how your skills and expertise make you the ideal new hire for one's company and organization. Your *overview* must illustrate why your skills and experience meet the needs of the organization.

Additionally, your work ethic and skill should complement the ethos of the company's values and objective as their employee. For example, your mission statement of your resume presents an opportunity for you to demonstrate your worth. A statement that both illustrates and showcases what added value you provide them. During your application process, think of your cover letter and the beginning of an interview as your opportunity to share your overview of what you uniquely bring to the table and how it will benefit the organization. Being able to flaunt your talents to the extent that you dazzle with a *"you need me"* attitude demonstrates confidence.

Interviews and Cross-Examination

Trying to convince the person on the other side of the table to hire you should be a breeze for any former debater. You have the skills to impress your potential employer in a job interview through the skills utilized in cross-examination. Debaters should keep in mind that the same skills used to ask questions to share more about what the opponent needs to know in each debate is similar in a job interview.

The interviewer is determined to find a candidate that fits the ideas and chemistry of their company or organization. The interviewer knows what they want to find in a potential hire. Therefore, the goal to win the interview starts with knowing your opponent and planning. Knowing your potential employer's mission statement, the company's history, its previous accomplishments, and other pertinent details help foster productive conversations. This means you should be *reading the room*. You should focus on the interview and think about ways you can connect with them while providing information about yourself that demonstrates you are the right candidate for the job. Questions such as, "Tell me a little about yourself?" should be a softball question you can hit out of the park as this open-ended question gives you the ability to flex and highlight the skills that make you both unique and valuable to them. Being able to plan by reading the room and knowing the answers they are looking for allows you to pivot your responses strategically.

Knowing your qualifications and the achievements that you reached because of your hard work and diligence in your craft is a great way to engage your interviewer. This approach allows you to tell a story about how experience in your craft helps complement the needs of the potential employer.

This is like knowing the philosophy of your arguments in relation to the judge's paradigm[1] when adjudicating debates. This skill enables you to adapt your answers to any unforeseen questions the interviewer throws at you. Knowing the company is like having familiarity with your opponent's case. This allows you to think about things from their perspective, identifying their needs, and being able to show how you can make their company or organization better.

Knowing Your Worth Is Like a Case Brief

As debaters prepare for a new topic, we spend our time toiling through the days and nights at our computer screens and researching the best possible answers for our positions. We work on identifying and resolving the most predictable flaws in our case, and we prepare responses to those arguments extensively by creating prewritten responses or *blocks*. We even go as far as to practice our arguments and strategies in public when we engage in mock debates and ultimately in the real-life debate.

Apply that preparation to your career development.

We can apply this same approach to the workforce. Understanding our worth in the workplace is essential to long-term career sustainability. However, it requires steps similar to your preparation for a debate round. First, you need to do a self-evaluation of your worth. Know whether you are being paid at value or if you are being underpaid and prepare to have that conversation. Those with debate experience can succeed in sustaining their worth and striving in their ability to know how much they are worth based on their perception of their experience, credentials, and skills that would legitimize their ask in salary. The ability to know what value you bring to a company or organization is the most important aspect of knowing your worth.

The Difference between Winning and Losing

One of the hardest realities about the exploration of finding a new job is the period of trial and error, perseverance through rejection. Just like a competitive debate, we can figure out the process of winning and losing debates. There is a clear distinction in terms of knowing the difference between winning and losing. Winning is more than the jubilant moment where success was achieved from defeating your opponent. Winning truly symbolizes that the strategy you crafted simply works. It is an affirmation that the strategy you designed, worked in its execution. Losing also holds symbolic meaning. Losing simply means the strategy you designed needs more refinement, but success can soon come. Knowing this during the process of finding a job can help you handle rejection along the way, can potentially help you figure out ways to establish changes in your job preparation that will help you land a future job, or may help you take the lead for a salary increase or an increase in job responsibility. But the preparation starts with accepting that it is going to be a process of trial and error.

Highlight Collaborative Skills

One of the most underutilized soft skills in the workplace is our collaborative skills. Debaters emerge from the activity with collaborative and team-building skills from the numerous practices where everyone congregates and practices debate. Conversations and deliberations occur, and instances of constructive feedback and criticism are often delivered in the session. Keep in mind that the preparation in learning from others enables individuals to know how they can contribute to the overall progress of the team.

First, think about the importance of a team practice. At a team practice, debaters are persistently engaged in developing strategies and solutions to argumentative problems that they will face at a debate tournament. As a result, debaters are writing potential answers, initiating research groups to cultivate evidence to support their claims in their arguments, and diligently practicing through oral communication such as practice speeches while defending their position through practice cross-examination drills. Second, during a debate round as you navigate the competition with your partner, you critically analyze the argumentative way of the land as you sift through the important arguments and strategies that must be executed against your opponent. You communicate to your partner on the expectations that each member must bring to the debate round, in order to win the ballot from your judge. Third, during the round you necessarily collaborate with your opponents to make sense of the issues presented in a debate. And finally, after the round as you hear the results from your debate, you collaborate with your judge to better understand what transpired, what worked well, and what you can improve upon.

Often, debaters are reminded that one person does not shape the success of the team overall. Instead, we all contribute to the overarching success of the team. When one person succeeds, we all succeed. The same can be applied to the workplace. By working collaboratively with your colleagues, you can demonstrate your strengths. In return, the contribution helps to establish progress in your company's goals.

Great Debaters Are Great Communicators

Paul Petrone, a writer for the prominent professional social media network LinkedIn, explains, "Strengthening a soft skill is one of the best investments you can make in your career, as they never go out of style."[2] Out of the top thirty skills accessed in terms of skills companies need the most, persuasion ranks second, just below creativity. In terms of its importance, the ability to persuade an audience to believe and understand your position establishes your ability to defend your ideas. In return, you create added value to the company with your ability to communicate. The ability to defend the ideas and thoughts of a particular company allows you to be valuable to any company or organization.

As debaters we hold a special talent in our ability to use rhetorical device to entertain thought, to move our audience into feeling a certain expression, and even change the mindsets of those who hold contrary options. This is not simply a gift but an asset that ensures added value to your work profile. Debaters perform constructive speeches in a debate round to establish statements that support and highlight your position. Depending on the audience, your intricate approach to word choice, the selective intonation of your voice, and even carefully selecting anecdotes all demonstrate your ability to connect with your audience in intentional ways. This deliberate approach creates a vision for your audience to follow and if you can get your audience to engage on the same level as you, then you are demonstrating attributes of a great communicator.

Conclusion

As debaters, we possess many talents that hold wealth outside of the debate space. Our activity instills within us aptitudes related to public speaking. Possessing the abilities of public speaking, research, and critical thinking gives us the upper hand in terms of your wealth in the workplace. Today, industries are looking for team collaborators and individuals who seek to improve themselves. Leaning into the skills taught in competitive debate allows you to demonstrate experiences that will ensure opportunities for career development. Our ability to elevate our worth in the job market first starts with knowing what we have in our rhetorical arsenal and putting it into practice.

Notes

1. *Editor's note*: A judge paradigm refers to how an adjudicator thinks debates should be evaluated, what they perceive debate should be, and their likes/dislikes regarding argumentation, stylistic delivery, and so on.

2. Paul Petrone, "The Skills Companies Need Most in 2019—And How to Learn Them," *Linkedin*, January 1, 2019, accessed August 3, 2020, https://www.linkedin.com/pulse/skills-companies-need-most-2019-how-learn-them-paul-petrone#:~:text=The%20Hard%20Skills%20Companies%20Need%20Most%20in%202019,...%205%20UX%20Design.%20...%20More%20items ...%20.

Section Two
Audience-Centered Debate

> If the decisions of judges are not what they ought to be, the defeat must be due to the speakers . . . Moreover (2) before some audiences not even the possession of the exactest knowledge will make it easy . . . Here, then, we must use . . . persuasion and argument . . . in order that we may see clearly what the facts are, and that, if another man argues unfairly, we . . . may be able to confute him.
>
> Aristotle, *Rhetoric*

Outsiders have a unique vision of what academic debate looks like. They picture teenagers in fancy suits. They imagine budding lawyers or politicians speaking eloquently in front of an audience. They see kids who are at the top of their class with high-powered schools in their future or on their resumes.

This image stems largely from the activity's traditional roots. In the beginning, students explored controversial topics with a focus on the audience in mind. They wore suits. They carried briefcases, legal pads, and fancy pens. They carefully projected a professional image at all times.

Debate mirrored a court of law. Although students debated issues of policy, the argumentation mimicked the practices of the judicial system. The affirmative team took on the role of prosecutor. They had the burden of proof to demonstrate that the status quo (or present system) was guilty beyond a reasonable doubt. They used five stock issues to prove their case.

They had to identify something harmful that existed in society. They had to show that the harm done was significant. They had to show there was something inherent about the system that caused the bad thing to exist. They had to propose a course of action by the federal government that fell within the boundary established by the annual debate topic. Finally, they had to show their proposal would solve the problem they identified.

The negative team, on the other hand, defended the present system. Their defendant—the status quo—was considered innocent until proven guilty. As such, they merely had to demonstrate there was reasonable doubt on any one of those five fronts: the problem may not exist, it might not be significant enough to warrant change, the system might not be the fundamental cause of the problem, the proposal might not be within the boundary established by the debate topic, or the proposed plan might not fix the problem.

All of this was presented with an emphasis on public speaking, and it was entertaining.

While many consider this performative style to be antiquated, out-dated, and part of a bygone era, it can still be found alive and well at tournaments in rural communities, much of the Midwest, and other regions where tournament directors recruit members of the local community to serve as judges, determining who wins and loses each debate. It also dominates formats such as Lincoln-Douglas and student congress, as well as international debating as practiced at the World Universities Debating Championships.

This approach created the backbone of an activity that fosters intellectual rigor.

5.
Inspired Learning

Gina Iberri-Shea

Now, more than ever, we see the real-world necessity of a populace versed in the critical thinking and civil discourse practiced in debate. These are requirements for a functioning democratic society. Based on what we have seen in media and political forums, it is easy to essentialize debate as a hostile game of competing assertions, filled with ad hominem attacks. Moving from this type of pseudo debate to the academic realm can be equally off-putting. Competitive debate, full of its own jargon, rules, and frameworks, can feel inaccessible to those outside the activity, as well as to communication scholars. This barrier to embracing and realizing all that academic debate has to offer, is not limited to outsiders. The very practices taught in debate, drive constant internal criticism and encourage questioning and weighing of its value at every level. I have seen this go in cycles, and it has driven many educators to move across formats in search of the Holy Grail of academic debate, a version that avoids the pitfalls that almost necessarily come with any competition. But it is precisely this type of academic competition that brings unique advantages.

Competition drives students to go beyond work that is merely adequate, to find and present the best and least disputable information, to search for holes in their own and other's argumentation, and to practice critical thinking throughout the process. While the students that are drawn to debate are certainly inclined toward academic discourse, pairing the adrenaline rush of competition with the creation of knowledge fosters a love of learning that is difficult to replicate in other environments. We see these benefits carry over into advanced study, career options, and leadership positions that move well beyond intercollegiate competition. Unless we are willing to relinquish those benefits, debate will not look like other forms of communication—and that's okay. Sure, there are things as a community we can do better. That will indefinitely be the case, and I wholeheartedly support productive interrogation. Debate should keep changing, improving, and becoming more accessible. But competition is the motivating factor for many, and much of the benefit is tied to the elements of the game that are not found in other communication practices.

I have had the not so unique experience of being part of several different debate communities, and I personally align with and enjoy some more than others. I was first introduced to debate through policy, Lincoln-Douglas, and the National Parliamentary Debate Association (NPDA). At the time, NPDA was the *break-away* format (at the collegiate level) with ambitions similar to what I saw later in British Parliamentary and then civic debate. My team currently focuses on British Parliamentary debate, which is a very audience-centered form that values many of the argumentation skills developed in policy and some of the rhetorical presence rewarded on more traditional debate circuits. One of the main differences is that policy debate leaves room to interrogate the starting assumptions of other communities.

Many of the elements we see across formats, and that are so fundamental to policy debate, vary simply in whether they are made explicit during argumentation and in the manner in which they are presented. Policy has been and is many things, and whether the debate centers on international relations or identity, it is a deep dive that probably involves heavy jargon and strategies to maximize the argumentative effort of the participants when confronted with time constraints. Policy itself has several variations in form, and this all-encompassing nature can be perceived as too much of an investment for the casual observer. But not every format of debate needs to appeal to a general audience.

Even though competitive policy is sometimes only understood by those fully immersed in the activity, policy debate is what I keep coming back to as an educator. Although there are claims that policy is less accessible, many argue that the range of argumentation and different styles of policy help to level access for participants. And access is precisely what drew me to debate. Policy debate has influenced and advanced my objectives both as a debate educator and in the English classroom, has clear applications in the real world, and has the power to affect change in individuals and communities. When asked the question, why debate, for me it is all the above.

The application of skills to the academic and *real world* was the shiny metal in debate that caught my eye. There are certain people who are naturally drawn to debate. *I was not one of them.* I had gone through life as an introvert coupled with anxiety associated with public speaking. This inability, or fear, of standing up, of speaking up, of standing out in any way, made everything feel more difficult. As a student who had to psych herself up for roll call on the first day of class, and rarely managed an audible "here," I was in awe of my peers who made it all look so easy. I watched as members of the debate team were able to stand out in class, take on leadership positions, and get better employment opportunities. They were so comfortable and so confident.

Although my anxiety evened as I grew older, I still felt the effort in what seemed effortless to everyone else around me. I was drawn to those that possessed these skills that eluded me, and there was an appeal to spending time with people who wanted to learn and asked interesting questions. Initially I entered the debate world for social reasons. Debaters wanted to always know more, not just about their major, but about the world. That was exciting, and the dynamic was unlike my experiences elsewhere. I enjoyed the debate community, even though I initially saw my role in it as peripheral.

It was not until I began to study teaching English and working with international students, that I decided to become an active participant in the debate community and recognized the impact debate had on my trajectory. Debaters held a privilege I had not known for most of my schooling, and I knew this advantage would be exponential for language learners. I was motivated to find ways to help my students access the benefits. In sum, I took part in an unplanned ethnography, learning debate to teach future students, and accidentally realizing benefits for myself.

As a student of teaching English to speakers of other languages, I saw policy debate as a tool to advance my objectives. Policy integrates academic skills beautifully. I have used forms of policy in my classroom and language learner environments because of the research and written preparation conducted prior to a live performance assessment. These are invaluable skills for success in academia. Students practice careful listening, notetaking, and critical thinking in an integrated way. Both the critical thinking and the communication literature support debate across the curriculum, and my experience has been particularly successful among language learners. Language skills improve because students are using language for specific purposes and working toward personal goals. Recognizing this, debate has influenced my professional interests. I piloted "English through Debate," a language learning curriculum, during my graduate studies, and have since developed it for secondary, postsecondary, and professional contexts. I have extended my application of debate education from the classroom to competitive programs, and this has ultimately guided both my research and career choices.

The same benefits seen in English courses apply to students outside of the humanities, who believe they are not adept at writing. Students on my competitive team apply the skills of debate to work across their courses. I have had dozens of STEM majors who attribute debate to significant improvement and ease in writing. One colonel in the United States Air Force and former debate team member told me that debate even made writing his PhD dissertation "easy." This is in addition to the obvious benefit these students have in class participation and presentation, which the more traditional style of policy certainly helps foster.

For the already successful and highly motivated students, debate's pairing of intensive academic study and the thrill of competition provides an opportunity to expand and fosters a love of learning. This consistently carries into real world endeavors and marks former debate students. At the Air Force Academy, every graduate I have talked to has told me that debate was one of, if not the most important thing they did during their undergraduate study, and that it had a significant impact on their future careers. Debate keeps you from becoming complacent, keeps you in touch with change and the future, pushes you to look at multiple sides of issues, and keeps you invested.

The debate community maintains bonds across institutions and generations. Not only do I believe this to be one of the most valuable aspects of the activity, but this has also heavily influenced my teaching philosophy. The two most influential mentors in my professional life have come from the debate community, and each has informed the way I approach the activity, my teaching, and my students. This has only been further supported by the close friends and colleagues I have on the debate circuit. I learned that it is not your best debater that is the most important, but it is the one that needs debate the most. My mentors showed me that giving back to the community is invaluable. I saw the bridges that could be built through debate, and I learned through observation what it means to lift others up. Although I have a long way to go, their perspective is what keeps me motivated and makes me want to be better.

Debate educators are often buried in administration and spend only a fraction of their time on what is seen in competition. The hours are brutal, and faculty often struggle in translating this type of academic work to university administrators and promotion boards. With this in mind, the question "why debate" is genuine. One answer is that the mentorship I have found within the community makes it worth it, and it is what has allowed me to maintain a passion for what I do.

I watch this community give back. I have colleagues working with debate in prisons, in underfunded schools, and in war-torn regions. As a debate educator, I get to learn from my students, have high level academic conversations about important issues, and engage interesting people from all over the world. I have seen debate, not only as part of competitive and language learning programs, but as part of government initiatives supporting nation building, new democracies, diplomacy, and antiterrorism efforts. It is not hyperbole to say that debate can affect real change in societies as well as in individuals.

In addition to my experiences with peers, mentors, and students in the United States, I have had the exceptional opportunity to work with students and educators from approximately fifty countries. As the world becomes more global, the impact of international communication practice and increased global awareness becomes even more critical. As an educator, I am rewarded when I listen to students from different nations negotiate the meaning of "unofficial education" or "women's rights." I am encouraged when I watch students from the United States talk about Ukrainian issues with their peers from both Ukraine and Russia, and then discuss it further over a cup of tea. I see them want to be better at recognizing their assumptions and communicating across cultures.

In the United States it is too easy for students to stay isolated. Sharing this activity helps to remove the *otherness*. Through our dissection of issues, we learn about the interests, desires, and needs of those who have different experiences than our own. Through our collaborative exploration of controversial issues, we learn to work with others who hold different points of view. Through our interactions we begin to build connections with individuals we may not have otherwise ever encountered in life. In short, debate develops connection on multiple levels. These experiences are not only of value to the students; they are constantly integrated into my world view. The debate community makes a difference.

When I adjudicate a round of debate, I am coming from the perspective of a teacher, and these opportunities allow me to appreciate variation and improve and develop my practice as a communicator in the world we share. My experience is not unique within the debate community. Academic, competitive debate inherently fosters cross-institutional dialogue. Throughout the year, students are judged by coaches, teachers, and topic experts from across the country, and in some cases the world. Our students gain access to expertise that extends well beyond their local environment. They often have opportunities to hear perspectives they would otherwise never encounter directly. The ability for students to learn from and interact with peers and faculty across institutions, to really expand their breadth of knowledge *and* perspective, is yet another advantage debate brings to the academic realm.

In short, debate increases opportunity and motivates learning. I am not pretending that there have not been problems. There will always be things we can do better, but I have benefited so much from debate, and I want to pass those benefits on to others. Debate has changed who I am and my ability to stand up. Debate affects how I see the world. Yes, there are shortcomings and valid criticisms of the activity, brought to light by voices I know from debate itself, and for whom I am grateful. But overall, what I see students and colleagues do through debate inspires me. Debate makes me want to be better.

6.
Debate and the College Experience

Nya Fifer

Debate was one of the best experiences of high school. It allowed me to interact with people from all over the country and build connections that I would not have otherwise been able to access. Not only this, but debate helped me develop real-world skills, talents, and insight that have greatly impacted my success as a speaker, a performer, and a college student. The skills I learned during my debate career were not simply supplementing those I learned in high school but building new ones that I had no clue would come in handy. As I sit here writing this while obtaining my undergraduate degree, I recall all the times I used or referenced debate. I can't think of a single presentation, paper, or lecture where I didn't think: Wow, doing debate helped me out. Although that may sound cliche, I cannot emphasize enough how much it has helped me. This chapter is dedicated to detailing how the resources, skills, and accolades I obtained during my high school debate career helped me from the time I applied to colleges to the conclusion of my sophomore year in college. Although my debate career ended only recently, I have already seen its profound impact on my college experience. It aided me tremendously as I applied for college, went through interviews, and navigated college-level academics.

Applications and Opportunities

When I was a high school debater, I remember hearing a member of my league telling us that colleges look at debate on an application as being more valuable than being a football player. I remember thinking: *Yeah right, no D1 college is going to choose a debater over an athlete.* At the time I was still a novice freshman debater, far too removed from the college application process to understand the truth in their statement. By the time I reached my junior year I began to understand. As I entered my first year as a varsity debater and began to apply for college, I found that a lot of colleges were recruiting students for debate and offered scholarships for students to debate on the college level. Most colleges offered scholarships of about two to three thousand dollars a year for students to debate on their teams. Having accolades in debate further bolsters one's likelihood of being scouted by college debate coaches. While I was debating in Missouri, I was scouted by many surrounding colleges and universities. However, doing well at the National Association for Urban Debate League Urban Debate Championship got me noticed by Georgetown, which was a super exhilarating experience.

Although debating has its benefits for getting noticed by college debate programs, it also is a good extracurricular to have on a college resume. It is a rigorous academic extracurricular, and it tells admissions counselors that you have engaged in relevant discourse about politics, social problems, and other current events. For example, some of the resolutions that I debated about included immigration, education, and international relations with China. These topics require a lot of prior knowledge and research to be able to debate about them. As a result, admissions counselors view it as a very prestigious sport.

Another major advantage is that debate offers more opportunities to win awards than other extracurriculars like athletics or noncompetitive clubs. With awards being given out at almost every tournament, it is unlikely that any student putting in effort won't win an award during their years as a high school debater. Success can certainly be an end, but each of the trophies or honors earned creates a picture of someone dedicated to their pursuit.

I listed *every* accolade I earned during my debate career, and while the more prestigious ones were more interesting to colleges, listing every single one created an impression of a well-rounded and successful competitor. When I got into Washington University in St. Louis, I remember that they listed some of the accolades of the incoming class before they released acceptance letters. I found my accolade on that list, and I cried from being so overjoyed: *national qualifying debater*, was among the accomplishments they decided to highlight. While I could go on bragging about that, the point is that accomplishments in debate really are prestigious, and hard work in debate can be incredibly valuable outside of the debate community.

On the topic of college applications, doing debate gives every debater something to talk about. In truth, having something of significance that you are passionate about is what colleges seem to be looking for from prospective students. Even now, almost two years removed from debate, I am extremely passionate and eager to talk about the niche topics I debated about and the fun stories that I picked up during my career as a debater. And these are *perfect* to use in application essays. Whether they are asking you to tell them about a high-tension moment in your life or to talk about something you are passionate about, debaters have no trouble conjuring up an answer drawn directly from their experiences. (*Be warned that debaters are skilled in the art of talking people to death, so make sure you have some time on your hands if you ever ask a debater to talk about debate.*)

Interviews

As a student's timeline for college applications continues, there are times when students are interviewing for internships, colleges, or scholarships that require a lot of well-developed speaking skills. To become a good debater, one must be just as good at answering questions during cross-examination as they are at monologuing during their speeches. Skills like quick thinking, being careful with diction and tone (*and having the ability to* BS) are all important when it comes to both debate and interviews. The ability to think quickly and expect the unexpected give seasoned debaters an edge in high stakes environments. An unexpected question that trips up an interviewee will almost always wash over debaters, and the insight into niche social topics that debaters usually have makes them seem far wiser than they are. (*Shh! Don't tell anyone!*)

Debaters are also far more likely to ask intentional questions of their interviewers that will probably shake them, which is a super important tactic if you want an interviewer to remember you. Making others think and question for themselves is a tool that puts the hard work on the audience instead of the speaker. Being able to do that is one of the most used skills in debate and one that a lot of people do not learn until they are far into their experiences in college or as adults. Whether that comes from asking questions or providing answers with rare insight, it will always set one above those who lack the skill. Speaking from personal experience in interviews, I felt like I always knew how to answer hard questions and what questions I could ask interviewers that would make them think. For example, during a scholarship interview when asked if I had any questions for them, I asked, "What is one thing you wish you could change about this university?" That simple question not only surprised my interviewers, but also gave me the opportunity to hear what members of the university thought about the in-stitution. Such an intentional question—that a debater wouldn't think twice about asking—told interviewers that I was considering the flaws and not just the beautiful parts of their institution in my decision-making process. It added a lot more depth to my character and my intentions than simply answering questions, without requiring me to do a lot of talking.

While I do not know if my questions and answers were just shocking or if they were wise, I do know that they were memorable. At the end of the day when the interviewers looked back through their notes having long forgotten most of the interview, I knew the unique insight that I had and the way that I engaged with their minds was what they would remember. I cannot say that I would have had those skills or developed such a strategy for interviewing if I had not debated.

College

Finally, debate has significantly influenced my experiences as an under-graduate student. One thing debate has done for me is that it has made me quite familiar with the research process. Cutting cards for debate is hard, so a debater who wants original evidence needs to be familiar with doing online research and narrowing it down to credible sources. Having that experience makes finding the right resources a fast and easy experience, and a lot of debate databases have good cards that can be used as a springboard for additional research. I personally have written several papers using the research that I started when I was a debater in high school.

Debate has also given me an enhanced understanding of how arguments should be broken down, which takes a lot of the guesswork out of writing an argumentative essay. In fact, I like to break down essays as if I was giving the first affirmative or negative speech in a policy debate, even if I'm not arguing about a policy. If I am arguing for something, I like to break down my argument with the problem (*Harm*), an explanation of why the problem has not and will not be solved (*Inherency*), and then offer my solution with various advantages (*Solvency*). Similarly, if I am arguing against something, I might attack the quality of my opponents' claims on any combination of those parts of their argument. The framing of debate rounds makes those three parts explicit, but I found that most arguments take on a similar format if you know how to look for it.

While I still find essay writing kind of hard to do, I will say that I do not have any trouble with speeches. When I first got into debate, I felt like I had a hard time with public speaking. I would be nervous before speeches and when I had to do presentations in class, and always felt like I had a hard time reaching a minimum time spoken. But as I progressed as a debater, I began to develop the ability to just go up in front of any crowd and speak about anything. Now, when I am required to present a topic in class, I rarely get nervous even if I do not feel confident in the material I am presenting, and I rarely need significant amounts of time to prepare for presentations. (*Having only five minutes of prep time for an entire debate will make anyone develop such a skill.*) In my opinion, this ability is by far my favorite out of all the skills I developed as a debater because it has made the often-dreaded college experience of having to present for a long period into something that feels so simple and natural. Conversely, now I have people tell me to slow down and that I talk like a debater, but to me, that is a much better problem to have than being lost and anxious during a presentation.

As I close out this chapter, I realize that not everyone will have the same experiences that I had as a debater. Some people will not be as involved in debate as I was while others will certainly do far more. And I want to point out that debate is not one of those sports where you will only get out of it what you put in. It will have something to offer everyone regardless of how much time they spend, how good they are, or how much they love debate. The opportunities, people, skills, and rewards that exist in the world of debate are available to everyone in different ways, but all of it is invaluable. I could not recommend debate enough, and I truly believe that it is a life-changing experience.

7.
Around the World and Back Again

Ashley Snookes

My final affirmative speech breezed by, but I had hit every point. I remember looking over to our opponents as I shared my trump card, the one piece of evidence I knew patched the hole in our case. I remember one of my opponents briefly closing their eyes. Several minutes later, my partner Megan got up, hitting one or two key points from the podium, and then pausing. Breaking tradition, she stepped out in front of the podium in white socks, no shoes, a scarf tied around her hips, and no suit jacket in sight. "Now, I'd like to tell you about my nephew," she said. I smiled and tensed, wondering how the judges would react to her unusual approach, and then relaxed as I read the interest in the room. She spent the last vital two to three minutes of her final speech telling a packed room a personal story as it related to our case. All eyes were on her, and it felt like no one dared to breathe until she finished.

That is how I remember the final policy debate round of the Alaska State Championship Tournament of 2003. At that time in Alaska, policy debate was practiced mostly in its traditional, stock issue and audience-centered form. Most debaters spoke at a conversational pace, wore suits, and packed around boxes of evidence, with some teams carrying larger boxes as an intimidation tactic (*we danced instead*.) My partner and I were from Sitka, a small island in Southeast Alaska that was rumored to have as many churches as it did bars and hair salons. While we came from a town of eight thousand and a high school of four hundred, we carried forward a tradition of success at the state championship for our small town. We were proud to bring home another winning title in policy debate.

As the excitement over winning diminished, we were asked whether we would attend nationals. The sheer cost of attendance alone deterred most teams from our region. On top of the cost, there were other considerations. We believed we could not be competitive nationally. Our traditional approach was quickly losing popularity, it seemed, to the contemporary, jargon-laced, fast-paced form of debate. Could the prestige and excitement be worth it? Was there something more to learn than what we had learned thus far? On top of that, Megan's mother was in her final weeks of life. She was battling cancer, and we knew those precious weeks at home were more important than the national tournament. Home turned out to be where we were both needed. That summer, my father was diagnosed with multiple sclerosis, and the life lessons I learned from Megan about facing the uncertainty of a parent's life journey helped me find my balance. I look back at that summer and see the choice as being one of attending and losing a few rounds before getting knocked out of the tournament, or staying and spending precious time at home, and I've never questioned our decision.

This was far from the end of the train ride for me in debate, however. In fact, it was just the beginning. As I look at what transpired from that summer forward, I realize that my experiences in high school debate gave me foundational life skills that have formed a core part of who I am today. The hard and soft skills I learned through debate, everything from public speaking to research, critical thinking to persuasion, seeing arguments from both sides, and working as a team: all of them carried forward into the next fifteen years of my personal and professional experiences. It has been a winding road, but it has taken me around most of the world and back again, on learning adventures that I never would have imagined during those final moments of the state tournament in the spring of 2003.

From high school, I went on to pursue a Bachelor of Science in political science with an emphasis in international relations. Debate made me keen to understand foreign policy. I came to see that decisions made by the United States impacted other people and nations abroad, and I wanted to better understand that relationship. At university, I continued my participation in debate and placed fourth at a national invitational competition. Sadly, the administration cut the competitive debate team my senior year in college. When the program was cut, I voluntarily started a student-run competition and pestered the administration to keep some form of the practice alive.

As I neared graduation, debate's impact on my interest in foreign policy and international relations led me to an internship with the United Nations. My research, critical thinking, and teamwork skills served me well during my internship; my passion for the practice led me to seek out the New York Urban Debate League's predecessor, the IMPACT Coalition, where I organized debate tournaments for inner-city schools in New York City. Job satisfaction was high: walking down the corridors of a tournament in action, seeing middle-school students whizzing through their policy speeches . . . I was exactly where I wanted to be, doing something that unquestionably mattered to me.

My search to understand the complex web of foreign affairs was far from over. I continued my journey east to Wales to study international security and development and to write a thesis on how United States policy affected the use of child soldiers internationally, under scholar and author Dr. Krijn Peters. My master's degree helped me continue to refine many of the skills I formed in debate, as professors held open debates and discussions in most of my classes. I prepared by completing the assigned reading, and then I would confidently, logically, and respectfully communicate what I thought were pressing considerations on everything from just war theory, to existential national security threats, to human rights policies. I also listened, asked genuine clarifying questions, and heard points of view that I had not considered. The deeper I dug into U.S. policy, the more I realized that no issue could be framed merely in black and white: the more I learned, the more I could see why certain decisions were made, and how incredibly difficult it is to solve international ethical and policy dilemmas. While I had not fully realized it at the time, my masters cracked my naïve vision of moving abroad and saving the (*third*) world. I was now an activist without an issue. Deeper than that, I was still hungry to learn about cultures, people, places, and the challenges that connect us all.

In 2011, I graduated with my master's, and world markets were still sluggish to hire new graduates. So, with my new husband, James (*whom I lovingly tease is worth all the debt I took out to study abroad for my master's, where I met him*), I went off to Japan to teach English, then on to Budapest, Hungary, to gain our teaching certifications, and finally off to Jeddah, Saudi Arabia.

I will never forget the moment my plane landed in Saudi. James had gone ahead of me since his passport was processed faster than mine. When the plane landed, everyone started pulling out thobes (men's robes), abayas (a black robe-like over-garment for women), and hijabs (women's head scarves). I had purchased an abaya online in advance and began to put it on over my jeans and t-shirt, my hands unsure of how to wrap the scarf as I tried to discretely watch other women to understand how to follow these new social norms. I stepped out of the plane, where it was hot, dry, and dark, and into a small, crowded bus. Men hopped up to offer me a seat and gave me more space than I ever had during rush hours on the A train in New York City. I made my way through the airport and to my husband who pulled up outside. As we drove home, I saw mosques with neon green lights, mangy street cats, plastic bags and wrappers littering the fences, and seemingly endless shish-kebab, falafel, and fruit stands, peppered with the black- and white-clad citizens and visitors of the country.

For the next two years, I taught political science, international relations, macroeconomics, and a host of other global topics at an all-women's university in Jeddah. In each class, I challenged my students to think critically, to view both sides of a topic, and to debate. For the final project in my international relations class, we held a small tournament, with teams from each class facing off in the final round. The women on the teams, from all over the Middle East, used evidence, logic, persuasion, and many of the other skills of traditional debate to make their points. I could not have been prouder of them.

My students grappled with many of the same issues facing American college students. They sought to understand the world at large, as well as their own, personal world. They were internally asking themselves what they believed about societies, religion, politics, and everything in between. We discussed Islam, feminism, socialism, terrorism, capitalism, and gender. My goal was to equip my students with the ability to research, analyze, and draw logical conclusions to guide their paths forward.

While I taught them, they taught me. If cultures could be placed on a spectrum, I think American, Japanese, and Saudi would form a Pythagorean triangle. Together, they formed vastly different approaches to the critical components of societies. Debate taught me to look from each angle. It taught me that the world is rarely black and white, and that no single perspective has all the answers. These lessons enabled me to see from others' perspectives as I immersed myself in these cultures. Life in each of these societies taught me different things. As I observed each, I began to draw my own conclusions about the structure and values I found to be most important, but also learned to remain a constant student of culture, societies, and the lived experiences of others that might be far different from my own.

After two years teaching at university and four years in education, I decided it was time for my career to take a turn. I had always wanted to understand political and economic systems from the inside, so my lessons in the classroom could be supported by a foundation of practical experience. My time as an intern with the United Nations opened a door to gain that experience. When an offer from a former co-intern came for me to lead research for the minister of economy of Saudi Arabia, Adel Fakeih, I accepted.

My primary role was to draft research papers on a variety of subjects for the minister and his advisors. Once again, I relied on the debate-built skills of critical analysis, research, summarizing and briefing on the most critical points, writing and speaking logically with confidence, and framing the issues concisely for a specific audience. The topics were wide-ranging and while getting to the root of the true question at hand was often challenging, the internal politics were even more challenging. I left after a year, and within two months of my return to the United States, international news headlines reported that Minister Adel Fakeih was one of the leaders to be locked in the Ritz-Carlton on charges of corruption by Crown Prince Mohammed bin Salman Al Saud. I never knew the specifics of the charges or the truth of them, but I was thankful to be home.

Through all of this, I was grateful to have James at my side. In marriage, there are most certainly times when I see a divergence between the conclusion of my rational brain, and that of my emotions. Being married to a partner that, though he never experienced debate himself, could concisely and kindly speak rationally, has left our family all the wiser. That fall, we welcomed our first child into the world and the following spring, we set out on our next adventure.

I decided to expand my understanding of the world once again by jumping to the other end of the triangle, this time from the macroeconomic view to the microeconomic. We took the ferry up to Juneau, Alaska (*not far from my home in Sitka*), where I joined a nonprofit focused on economic development in Southeast Alaska. In my role, my background in education and economics are combined. I spend much of my time individually coaching clients or organizing and delivering training sessions for small groups, all focused around starting or growing small businesses in Southeast Alaska.

Once again, I find the most satisfying parts of my day come from seeing clients learn and grow through researching and planning their business, a process not entirely different from the cases I built as a debater (*with the addition of some financial modeling and accounting*). I work with them through a process of researching, writing, analyzing, finding the gaps, and researching again. The resulting business plan guides their path as they build businesses that define some of the daily experiences of community members throughout this rugged, rural, island-strewn region of Alaska.

I knew when I returned to Alaska that life would not be complete without giving back to the activity that taught me so much, and so I have also coached the local debate team with two other outstanding coaches for the past three seasons. While the form of debate in our region now focuses on public forum instead of the traditional policy debate I engaged in, I see similarities between this format and the audience-centered approach of policy that I grew up with, in terms of its practice and lessons learned. What I saw as a game and competition in high school, I now see in the bigger picture of life. Tournaments build resiliency, giving students real-life experiences over and over again in receiving challenging feedback, providing the opportunity to practice and be rewarded when they improve, and building their teammates as they grow. The lessons I give them in argumentation ring in my head as I engage in work meetings and am reminded that every tool can continue to be refined and implemented for growth, and the circle of learning continues.

My journey has been far from predictable or straight, and the curves and twists of my journey have brought greater adventures than I ever imagined. Debate taught me to look for the learning opportunity in every bend, and to push myself to build skills and engage in experiences that stretched me. My professional goals and aspirations drive me to continue to learn, engage, build, and grow. I have had many years of experience applying the tools and skills I developed in debate to the activities in my own professional and personal life. I am grateful for the person it has helped me to become, and as I tell each new team I coach, I firmly believe there is no better high school activity for learning some of life's most important skills. I look forward to continuing along this winding road. It has been a beautiful journey.

8.
Policy Debate in a Postmodern Society

Benjamin Collinger

In July 2020, *Harper's Magazine* published a prominent "Letter on Justice and Open Debate." The letter, signed by dozens of public intellectuals ranging from Francis Fukuyama to Margaret Atwood, warned of a rising illiberal tide. Contemporary movements for racial justice are crucial, the authors noted, "but this needed reckoning has also intensified a new set of moral attitudes and political commitments that tend to weaken our norms of open debate and toleration of differences in favor of ideological conformity."[1] The letter became immediately controversial. Though its spirited defense of argument and persuasion represent classically liberal values, the critique also evoked tired commentary about political correctness.

Elaborating upon the *Harper's* thesis, *The Economist* highlighted a parallel "new ideology of race."[2] Adherents to this ideology, the authors wrote, reject the liberal notion of progress and impose ideas through intimidation and power. "Not the power that comes from persuasion and elections, but from silencing your critics, insisting that those who are not with you are against you, and by shutting out those who are deemed privileged or disloyal to their race."[3]

These critiques contain some merit because political discourse is often acrimonious. Ideology-reinforcing media ecosystems have not helped. However, the outcry from thinkers like the *Harper's* signatories and *The Economist* seems to be an overreaction (at best) or made in bad faith (at worst) in response to the alleged illiberal tactics of activists. The critique is a poor response to the substance of antiracism and draws false equivalencies with the practices of autocrats abroad. A civil, reasoned, and well-argued debate would undoubtedly be preferable in political controversies. Faith in such an ethic represents why this volume sits in your hands.

In any case, politicians and constituents alike must weigh their argumentative strategies against the limits of social network algorithms, political institutions, and the patience of those they love. As a result of dynamics like negative partisanship, divisive strategies often pay short-term dividends while careful argumentation and coalition building do not.[4] Our country's unique civic moment begs new questions of acceptable political strategies and speech.

In this environment, what is the role of scholastic policy debate? How might the activity prepare ethical and skilled students to enter a world of seemingly unbreakable polarization? This chapter will argue that for all its flaws, debate provides necessary answers. Competitive policy debate, if equitably taught and funded, prepares students to shape the boundaries of twenty-first century discourse in valuable ways. The activity prizes persuasion and helps students develop critical thinking skills to excel in our postmodern political society.

Competing Truth Regimes

The *Harper's* letter drew from a rich tradition of classical liberalism. In fact, its thesis is closely related to one strand of modern political thought: John Stuart Mill's *On Liberty*. As it relates to freedom of expression, Mill cautioned that individuals need protection not only against abusive government, but also against a society's prevailing opinion or feeling. "Society," Mill explained, "practices a social tyranny more formidable than many kinds of political oppression, since . . . it leaves fewer means of escape, penetrating much more deeply into the details of life, and enslaving the soul itself."[5] In other words, the social norms that define truth-seeking and debate—what is examined, by whom, and in what medium—often matter far more than laws. Politics and law may be downstream from culture. Mill's argument is premised on the need for truth-seeking, which he said requires contrasting opinions for several reasons: ideas compelled to silence may be true; silenced arguments may be partly true and can add needed context to the prevailing opinion; even verified truths must be contested; doctrine will be worthless without contest and debate.

While traditional policy debate is classically liberal and largely follows Mill's approach to truth-seeking, debaters also learn that truth is socially contingent. The postmodern French philosopher Michel Foucault might translate Mill's theory of social tyranny into a society's "general politics of truth—that is, the types of discourse it accepts and makes function as true; the mechanisms and instances by which each is sanctioned; the techniques and procedures accorded value in the acquisition of truth; the status of those who are charged with saying what counts as true."[6] Foucault and Mill agree that defining truth is one of society's powers. Yet Foucault does not separate truth from the power that produces it. He argues that truth is neither outside of nor lacking in power. "Truth is a thing of this world: it is produced only by virtue of multiple forms of constraint. And it induces regular effects of power."[7] As a result, actors have immense incentives to gain power regardless of a more academic search for "truth."

Different truth regimes are omnipresent in American life. As political parties become more ideologically homogeneous, their associated cultural, religious, and geographic identities have merged. Identities have also coalesced along various demographic lines. One example of the consolidation is that there are almost zero conservative Democrats or liberal Republicans today (as there once were), while race and residence are also key predictors of political party. "Our political identities have become political mega-identities. The merging of the identities means when you activate one you often activate all, and each time they're activated they strengthen," explained journalist Ezra Klein.[8] The activation of political identities often means there are fewer incentives for individuals to present a careful argument or engage in a debate with people who disagree.

Moreover, voters in such a polarized dynamic do not behave as Mill might expect. Christopher Achen and Larry Bartels have found that "even the most informed voters typically make choices not on the basis of policy preferences or ideology, but on the basis of who they are—their social identities."[9] The weakening of common identities has major implications for debate and discourse writ large. Few actors hold the same values or ideological framework from which a debate can begin, and even fewer deeply consider policy alternatives. However, the existence of polarization is no reason to reject scholastic debate as a tool unfit for our times. The collegial environment it cultivates for young students is one of the few places that they are compelled to disagree respectfully, engage rigorously in policy discussions, and build empathy for people with opposing identities or worldviews.

Valuing Debate amid Polarization

What is the value of debate if citizens come from opposing truth regimes? Although it is not immediately obvious, policy debate offers participants a skill set capable of confronting the problem. First, the activity teaches participants to establish the limits of debate and the permissibility of certain words and arguments. Debaters dispute the meaning of the season's resolution, or topic, and the words it contains. They must jostle over the purpose of the judge, what constitutes a productive debate, and critiques of their own premises. Affirmative and negative teams can even decide *whether* they should be compelled to defend the side of the topic that the tournament assigned. Even in its simplest stock issue form, policy debate prepares students to defend their interpretation of the boundaries for debate, which is excellent training for a world of constantly shifting political discourse. The fact that no framework is completely immovable is an indelible contribution toward a student's intellectual development. Openness to innovation and change partly forms the basis of design thinking: a process entrepreneurs and many other disciplines use to create new products and identify society's most pressing challenges. Never assuming a popular framework is unassailable proves extremely valuable in the workplace, too.

Second, the activity rewards debaters who persuade different audiences and teaches them how to assess risk. For example, when confronted with a panel of three judges where two view themselves as mock policymakers (i.e., rather than academics or lay members of the community), both teams know to converge upon a plan and policy-focused round. Debaters learn when persuasion can win and when they should take a risk with novel argumentation or rhetoric. I have personally used this framework to adapt my language not only in debate rounds, but also to the diverse audiences in my career: from worker cooperative participants and social justice advocates to business leaders. Such adaptation informs the calculus that many activists, politicians, and businesspeople have used to great success. The experience often teaches students when it is strategic to advocate outside the boundaries of the prevailing opinion and when it is not. Learning when to lead change and how to build political capital within a community provides value both in debate rounds and outside of them. Even in a world of cascading polarization, students learn to evaluate policies fairly and disagree in a civil manner.

I enjoyed each of these positive outcomes of policy debate in my life. Policy research prepared me for investigations in collegiate history projects, my journalistic endeavors, and writing clear business memos. I used the skills to pitch a journalism startup that reached over thirty universities, write persuasive essays, and even market an artificial intelligence company. Without the experience of scholastic debate, I would not have had the same practice evaluating the credibility of media sources nor the habit of balanced news consumption. My ability to quickly formulate ideas and speak extemporaneously plays as well in the corporate boardroom as it did within scholastic debates. Understanding new audiences has been useful as I began my career leveraging a business-friendly conservatism to advocate for racial equity in entrepreneurship. Each experience trained me to question my own assumptions and make contributions toward a more equitable community.

Illiberal Antiracism?

While policy debate has immense potential to help students confront the challenges described in this article, it also exists within a broader context of inequity and occasional hypocrisy. Many debaters have attempted to lead change and have been met with misguided opposition. I think of my traditional, conservative high school circuit's response to what has been called *performance debate* (a racially coded term often used in reference to Black students using personal stories to illustrate structural racism with less adherence to argumentative convention). In reality, these debaters were often skilled advocates for racial justice who critiqued the prevailing argumentative frameworks. My contemporaries (and I, early in my debate career), echoing themes from the *Harper*'s letter, would say that *performance debaters* forced false choices and unethical responses from their opposition. Many in our district felt such approaches were illiberal and antithetical to what they understood as debate. On the contrary, unconditional opposition to debaters who challenged "tradition" was often guided by racial bias: many forms of policy debate—especially plan-focused, audience-centered forms—do value a form of physical comportment (dress and appearance), speaking (dialect, vocabulary, cadence, and enunciation), and data (research and types of evidence) that can have exclusionary effects on Black and brown students. Perhaps more to the point, the activity's occasional failures to engage the arguments and respond to the needs of students represent a clearer example of illiberalism than their arguments in the first place. Conservative circuits ought to open themselves to new norms in policy debate that allow the activity to truly realize the values it professes.

A more inclusive policy culture need not weaken the value of open debate or create ideological conformity. Critically, scholastic debate's future as a forum to engage one's community and form a well-rounded social consciousness depends on inclusion. School districts ought to engage more students and judges of color (i.e., via scholarships for summer debate institutes, intentional mentorship programs, and representative marketing in recruiting), while lawmakers could make structural reforms (i.e., revenue streams). Debate is well-suited to an inclusive pivot and can be guided intentionally by coaches attuned to disparities in the activity. It is precisely this malleability that will prepare students to shape the boundaries of discourse among the diverse stakeholders in their lives.

Open Debate and Justice

The challenge of polarization and political conflict cannot be confronted without broader societal reform (i.e., a stronger local media ecosystem and fairer apportionment of power), but the approach that debate can teach will produce citizens capable of driving progress. As Foucault might note, the project of argumentation in a postmodern political world is a matter of building the case for a new power establishment. No activity provides students with better preparation to create such new power establishments than debate. It rigorously prepares students to engage ethically with diverse stakeholders regardless of where their careers lead them. As debaters know well, justice and open debate will not end because some actors have opted for an illiberal political strategy: it will end if citizens do not know how to argue for and lead an alternative.

Notes

1. *Harper's Magazine*, "A Letter on Justice and Open Debate," July 7, 2020, accessed August 17, 2020, https://harpers.org/a-letter-on-justice-and-open-debate/.

2. *Economist*, "The New Ideology of Race: And What Is Wrong with It," July 9, 2020, accessed August 17, 2020, https://www.economist.com/leaders /2020/07/09/the-new-ideology-of-race.

3. *Economist*.

4. Jill Lepore, *If Then: How the Simulmatics Corporation Invented the Future*, (New York: W.W. Norton and Company, 2020), 32–52. Among other sources, see Lepore's discussion of the Eisenhower-Nixon campaign and influence of advertising and divisive strategy of presidential politics.

5. John Stuart Mill, *On Liberty* (United Kingdom: Project Gutenberg, 1859), https://www.gutenberg.org/files/34901/34901-h/34901-h.htm, United Kingdom: Project Gutenberg, January 10, 2011.

6. Paul Rabinow and Nicholas Rose, eds., *The Essential Foucault: Selections from the Essential Works of Foucault, 1954–1984* (New York: The New Press, 2003), 316.

7. Rabinow and Rose.

8. Ezra Klein, *Why We're Polarized* (New York: Avid Reader Press, 2020), 70.

9. Christopher Achen and Larry Bartels, *Democracy for Realists: Why Elections Do Not Produce Responsive Government* (Princeton: Princeton University Press, 2016), 4.

Section Three
Progressive Debate

As for one who is choosy about what he learns . . . we
shall not call him a lover of learning or a philosopher,
just as we shall not say that a man who is difficult about
his food is hungry . . . We shall not call him a lover
of food but a bad feeder . . . But we shall rightly call a
philosopher the man who is easily willing to learn every
kind of knowledge, gladly turns to learning things, and
is insatiable in this respect.

Plato, *The Republic*

Eventually, the landscape of debate shifted dramatically. No longer were
students focused on persuading members of the lay community to vote
for them at the end of the debate round. Tournaments began relying on
professionally trained judges—mainly coaches and alumni—to populate
the judging pool.

This meant that argumentation reigned supreme. No longer were
students required to debate in suits. My college days in the 1990s found
debaters in flannel and jeans or in shorts and flip flops.

Debaters stopped mirroring a court of law's judicial model of debate and began pursuing a legislative model of debating. This involved
evaluating costs and benefits. It opened the door to more issues being
explored within a debate round. The complexity of thought skyrocketed.
New argumentative structures developed. It was no longer enough to

evaluate the merits of a proposed plan in a vacuum. There were unintended consequences or disadvantages that could be triggered by the course of action. There were opportunity costs of choosing a course of action, so we might prefer a counterplan to make the world a better place. A team might use harmful language when speaking or flawed methodologies when constructing their ideas, and therefore might be critiqued. As such, multiple disciplines were interrogated within debate rounds, further encouraging the use of *professional judges* while discouraging lay people from observing and judging debates.

No longer were students required to engage in public speaking. The arguments explored were incredibly nuanced. Jargon permeated speech. The clock became the enemy. How could one truly explore these topics in an hour and a half, let alone a speech that lasted a mere eight minutes? Debaters found a solution. They spoke faster and developed more jargon. Rather than a public speaking rate of roughly 150 words per minute, debaters began speaking at 200 . . . 300 . . . 450 words per minute.

For several decades, this style dominated the landscape, and largely still does in college and on the high school's national circuit. While initially taking root in policy debate, it has spread to other formats such as Lincoln-Douglas, public forum, and the National Parliamentary Debate Association. It challenges students, coaches, and judges to think in new ways. To stretch themselves. To identify connections between ideas and between communities of people. To outsiders, it seems like gibberish. It seems absurd. But, to those who practice it, it is a beautiful thing.

9.
Defending Policy Debate

Shawn F. Briscoe

Many coaches have complained that there is a problem with policy debate.[1] At professional development conferences, in judges' lounges at tournaments, and even in articles published in journals devoted to speech and debate, coaches have detailed the trends within the activity that are destroying or, at least, disrupting its merits. In December 2009, the NSDA's *Rostrum* featured an article by Dan O'Rourke that detailed a few of the common complaints or "proofs" that policy debate is either dead or well on its way to the grave.[2] Perhaps the most persistent complaint is the prevalence of speed or talking fast. One such article written by Hall of Fame coach Bob Bilyeu horrifyingly called upon coaches to intervene in debates and vote against teams that employed speed, simply because they chose to speak quickly.[3] No competitive format is perfect, but I believe policy debate offers numerous benefits because of rather than despite some of the major criticisms. Other chapters in this book explore those benefits. Here, I challenge some of the fundamental assumptions upon which many of the charges rest, specifically address the principal complaints lodged by critics, and explore some of the areas we must address regarding the current state of policy debate.

First and foremost, I see value in the practice of speed or rapid-fire delivery in policy debate. I also see value in the argumentative structures known as disadvantages, counterplans, and kritiks. All can be quite beneficial to the activity. Together, they help develop students' minds to think critically, analytically, and quickly. I personally reaped the benefits of the activity steeped in those practices during my six-year stint as an officer in the military. I have seen my peers from the Air Force Academy policy debate team benefit intellectually and professionally, as well. I have seen my former students at high schools in Florida, Alaska, and Missouri reap those same benefits. I believe the "problems" with policy debate can be attributed to other phenomena. At the same time, they can be overcome through the efforts of teachers and coaches.

Fatal Assumptions

Many critiques of policy debate rest on one or more of three flawed assumptions. First, coaches and judges returning to the activity contend that it has changed so much that it is no longer recognizable to those who debated ten, twenty, or thirty years ago. I do not believe this is the case. I have been debating since I was a freshman in high school in the fall of 1990. At that time, I competed on the local circuits of Missouri—a circuit dominated by lay judges and traditional coaches. Upon graduation, I competed for the Air Force Academy during the CEDA and NDT merger. From 2002 to 2006, I coached Fort Walton Beach HS as we traveled the national circuit to tournaments such as Harvard, Glenbrooks, Wake Forest, and Emory. From there, I moved to Alaska, where I coached on a local circuit comprised almost entirely of judges not familiar with policy debating. Then, I served as the program director for the Saint Louis Urban Debate League, which had its own unique blend of styles. On the face of it, one might say that these experiences were radically different.

They were not.

Despite the variances in speed and argument selection, what constitutes a solid debate remains the same. At the most basic level, a good debater still makes a claim, supports it with facts or evidence, and makes comparisons between her arguments and those of her opponents. At a more nuanced level, the qualities of an argument are still the same. Are the logical connections between points formed? Are the *stock elements* of a particular argument present? In fact, these elements do not really change across time or formats.

Whether I reflect upon my high school years debating in front of Missouri's community volunteers, listen to my students engage their parents on whether they should be allowed to attend yet another tournament, witness the holistic debating of international teams on the world debating circuit, or reflect upon the points that were persuasive in staff meetings in the military, these arguments have not changed. The fundamentals upon which a case is built and the modes of deconstructing them are the same; only the titles, rates of delivery, and scope of ideas have changed.

In addition, many critics point to the decreased number of competitors taking part in the activity. Again, there is a fatal assumption in using this as proof of their argument. For the most part, these individuals competed in the 1960s or 1970s. At that time, there was only one major format of debate available to students. With the advent of Lincoln- Douglas, public forum, student congress, world schools, and Big Questions as competing debate events, it necessarily decreases the number of students engaged in policy debate.[4]

At roughly an hour and a half, a single debate round takes longer than all but congress. Its speeches are also longer than those of any other format. This scares many students to other events. As a format, it is the most likely to incorporate knowledge of the political process, international relations, philosophy, sociology, science, and *more* within the confines of a single round. Conversely, other formats tend to treat only one or two of these aspects at a time.[5]

Compounding these factors, many schools rely upon someone with a background in English or theatre to run their debate programs. As someone new to the activity, policy debate seems just as daunting to them as it does to their students. In some cases, this is because they have the same reservations about the length of the activity as the students, or they have a lack of subject experience in the social sciences. In other cases, they are simply scared off by the advice given to them by other coaches as they enter the world of forensics, who tell them that policy is broken, scary, or evil.

Finally, many critics compare their evaluation of a mediocre or poor round to their ideal image of what a debate is supposed to look like. In other words, I freely admit there are poor debaters who utilize speed as a strategy to spread their opponents out of the round. However, there are also exceptionally good debaters who use speed to add depth of analysis to their arguments. A bad team or a bad debate should not represent the entire activity. In other words, when lodging a blanket criticism of trends within the debate community based on examples of teams who abused their opponents through rapid-fire delivery of an incoherent idea (or a coherent one that the speaker did not understand), we should remind ourselves that bad debates have always existed.

I remember horrible debates when competing in front of lay judges in Missouri. Consider the eloquent speaker who lacks a coherent thesis and fails to engage his opponents' ideas, yet mesmerizes the inexperienced lay judge and picks up the ballot. Similarly, think of the disorganized debater who has not thought through the issues, but muddles the round so badly the judge does not know how to evaluate the round. Finally, consider the student who asks question after question about minute details without ever managing to string together an actual critical thought. These are not indicative of high-quality argumentation.

Obviously, a good debater transcends these failures. But so too does the good debater transcend the poor debating of someone who uses speed as a strategy or does not understand the arguments they present. Case in point: at the 2007 Harvard Invitational, I took a policy team whose only experience with debate was extremely traditional and mostly conducted in front of parents and teachers. They had never confronted speed, generic disadvantages, kritiks, counterplans, or narratives. They stuck to the basics and argued from the place with which they were comfortable. The end result? A 4–3 record. The point is twofold. First, we cannot judge the entire activity based on a few bad examples—surely our experiences in debate have taught us this much. Second, debate is not corrupt; it still values quality discourse—it always has. The main difference is the rate at which those arguments are presented, the amount of depth that can be presented by good debaters, and the names of the specific twists on old arguments. In other words, an unthinking, uncritical team will almost always lose to a team that thinks critically about the issues and presents those ideas in clearly articulated responses.

The Usual Suspects

Nevertheless, there are a few specific attacks that have been levied against policy debate in its contemporary form: it lacks academic application, it has become reliant on jargon that only a policy debater can understand, and it has devolved to focus on argumentation rather than education.[6] Let us address those critiques one at a time.

First, many argue that policy debate is no longer academically applicable. Let us unpack that criticism. Many, like O'Rourke, have conflated the concepts of *academic* or *education* with that of *communication*. Look at the phrases he uses to illustrate his point: "No judge would tolerate it in a courtroom . . . Could this example of Policy Debate in any way be considered effective communication?"[7] As for the actual meaning of this argument, I acknowledge that policy debate does not currently prepare one for public speaking engagements in the way that extemporaneous speaking or original oratory do.

Nevertheless, it does teach students how to conduct research, make connections between lines of argumentation, think quickly on one's feet, and present ideas in an organized and coherent fashion. All these skills translated perfectly to my involvement in command staff meetings in the United States Air Force and as a classroom teacher. Furthermore, the process of analyzing a policy debate topic from multiple paradigms (traditional policy, critical perspectives, and so forth) over the course of an entire season helps students understand that these issues and perspectives do not occur in a vacuum.[8] In addition, the activity inherently pushes students to listen closely to what their opponents say. Ultimately, this helps them understand *the other's* perspective. In the end, debate is about finding commonality in our differences, so that matters of true importance—outside the debate round—can be addressed in a constructive manner.

Second, many argue that policy debate is corrupt because it has become too reliant on jargon or too complex for the average student. On some level, this might be the case. Nevertheless, critics such as O'Rourke have misidentified the jargon that has made the activity complex. He specifically identifies terms such as eco-fem and Heidegger as "policyspeak."[9] More recently, debaters explore issues like biopower, neoliberalism, settler-colonialism, Afro-pessimism, and critical race theory. Policy debaters did not develop those terms, names, or concepts. They are written about extensively and studied in academia around the world. Admittedly, however, policy debate—and all debate—has a dizzying array of terms used by the participants: inherency, link, brink, perm, alt, and topicality; most of which have been around for decades.

Still, the question remains, is policy debate complex? Has it evolved to the point where debaters no longer evaluate a plan in a vacuum—thus, creating a web of interconnected concepts and ideas? Does it have its own language? In reference to the first question, I say, yes it has. But, I also ask, *why is that bad?*

As a football fan, I see parallels with that sport. I do not think the advent of the forward pass, triple option, West Coast offense, or spread option undermined its beauty as a sport. Nor have they destroyed the merits of team sport or fitness. To the contrary, I think most football fans and athletes would concur these developments improved the sport. The evolution of an activity should not be viewed as inherently bad. Rather, we should evaluate the merits of the change not on knee-jerk reactions, but upon reflection after seeing what those developments bring to the table.

To the second question on whether policy debate has its own specialized language, of course it does—and always has. We should also remember why jargon develops within a field of study or activity. It develops as a form of shorthand between people who communicate regularly on specific concepts. Thus, it eases the communication process between people within the activity. However, if debaters fail to adapt to a judge who lacks background in that world, then they have failed to communicate effectively. This is no different from a physician who uses medical terminology when speaking to her colleagues, but then must adapt that language when speaking with a patient.

To O'Rourke's broader point, if we wish to use jargon and complexity as our standards for evaluating the merits of a field of study, then we may need to ask ourselves why we maintain courses in physics, calculus, and economics in our high school curriculum. They are also complex and filled with their own specialized vocabulary. Interestingly, they historically have the fewest number of enrollees within the science, math, and social sciences departments. That does not make them bankrupt or worthless when placed alongside integrated science, consumer math, and so forth. Isn't the point of an educational endeavor to push oneself beyond the comfort zone, to learn how to learn, to make connections in ways that were previously unheard of for that individual? Policy debate, like the aforementioned courses, does just that.

Finally, critics of contemporary policy debate argue that it is focused more on argumentation than education. I think this statement takes a too-narrow view of the activity. It cannot be defined by a single round. Rather, it must be looked at holistically. In other words, I cannot contend I understand physics because I can calculate $v=d/t$ or even a single lesson in a physics class. The educational experience of debate starts when the students are introduced to the topic, progresses through the season as students engage myriad debaters on a virtual plethora of arguments, and ends long after they graduate and move on to whatever path their lives take.

Contrary to the criticisms that claim competitive debate is devoid of academic merit, the research paints a very different picture. At the college level, a 1990s-era meta-analysis evaluated the effects of participating in public speaking classes, argumentation classes, and competitive speech and debate teams on critical thinking. The findings indicated "all methods of communication skill improvement generate gains in critical thinking. The largest effect, however, was observed for competitive forensic participation."[10] Admittedly, this study was generally applicable to speech and debate. However, additional studies specifically related to students' participation in policy debate bear similar results.

A ten-year study from 1997 to 2006 of the Chicago Urban Debate League identified myriad tangible gains for students. This extensive study found that "debaters and non-debaters did not differ significantly in terms of concentration in poverty" and other "school-level characteristics."[11] Nevertheless, debaters were "19% more likely to graduate from high school"; "after accounting for selection bias," debaters' achievement of college-readiness scores on the ACT relative to their peers was "statistically significant"; and gains in GPA over their high school careers outpaced that of their peers.[12] This particular study has been analyzed multiple times to account for other variables, but still continues to demonstrate additional gains for debaters.[13]

Finally, a more recent ten-year longitudinal study of more than 84,000 elementary and middle school students in Baltimore shows similar results. Like the Chicago study, the researchers accounted for other variables and still found that debaters had larger gains (than their peers) in GPA, reading scores, math scores, and school attendance.[14] Time and time again, research shows us that participation in competitive debate has real academic value.

Legitimate Concerns

While I believe many of the criticisms of contemporary policy debate are rooted in flawed assumptions or are otherwise inaccurate in their attacks, I acknowledge that the activity is not devoid of legitimate criticism. In fact, I have seen several trends over the years that can easily be corrected with some adjustments in coaching strategies. These concerns are analogous to the previously mentioned examples of the gifted orator who lacks a thesis or coherent point. That is, there are practices that work against the educational merits of the activity and give rise to the concerns presented by many of the activity's critics. In a previous version of this article, I discussed some of these practices in delivery that cause concern. For example, I discussed the lack of clarity due to insufficient signposting and lack of organic clash due to overreliance on prewritten overviews and hyperspecific frontline answers. Instead, I will look at two larger, philosophical issues that require our attention.

Issue 1: Educator Apprehension

As policy debate has gotten faster, more technical, and more interconnected, coaches and judges have chosen to remove themselves from the equation. Because they do not like the trends within the activity or do not feel qualified to teach in that environment, they decided to focus elsewhere. This creates a compounding problem in which the activity becomes increasingly insular.

It is my longstanding belief that any academic pursuit suffers in isolation. As the discipline becomes more homogeneous, it loses impetus to grow. It is no longer challenged. It is no longer forced to adapt to differing perspectives. Thus, as coaches and judges remove themselves, the activity becomes dogmatic and accelerates its move along a singular path. We very much need debaters, judges, and coaches with differing approaches to the activity. Only when they intermingle do we truly have an opportunity for growth.

Alongside this development has been a move by coaches to rely on outsiders to run their policy debate programs. Again, whether they have a distaste for the format or are concerned they lack the expertise to teach it, they call upon recent graduates to enter their classrooms and teach their students. Unfortunately, this can be harmful to the format.

This is ultimately an educational activity. It is one thing to invite a guest speaker into our classroom or to have a parent or student aide working alongside us. It is something else entirely to hand our classroom over to someone else. As a teacher, I might invite a salesperson, a doctor, a chemist, or a pilot into my classroom to provide unique insight for my students. My kids' teachers in elementary school occasionally had a parent aide who assisted with instruction. However, none of us were willing to invite someone into the room and let them run the day-to-day development and implementation of lesson plans.

These recent graduates are a wonderful resource. However, they are not educators. By and large, they do not have the mindset of an educator and they rarely have experience with effective methods of instruction. More likely, they have the mindset of a competitor. Many of them lack the perspective of hindsight to understand the real benefits of the activity. Many of them hope to live vicariously through current debaters, to extend their own competitive careers. Thus, rather than teaching younger students how to debate effectively, they try to inject themselves into the debate; they strive for wins in the short term rather than growth over the long term. In turn, this contributes to many of the concerning issues such as overreliance on prewritten strategies and other toxic attitudes.

Issue 2: Toxic Attitudes

The second major problem is the most destructive: a belief that competition is the ultimate identifier of success. Far too many individuals wrap themselves in the competitive nature of the activity, losing sight of the elements of community and education that make it meaningful.

While competition certainly serves as a motivating force, too much emphasis on it is corrosive. In its least damaging form, this hyper focus on competition manifests as cutthroat struggles for championships and trophies where opposing teams view themselves as enemies rather than partners in an educational and competitive framework. Debaters immersed in that world take the wrong lessons away from the activity—that it is only a game. They likely miss the more significant lessons the event offers participants.

In addition, it gives rise to the notion that there is a *right way* to debate. Thus, certain performative styles are valued by the competitors and recent graduates—who serve as volunteer coaches and judges—over alternative approaches to the activity. One need look no further than social media following the national championship tournaments to see this attitude on display: when debaters disparage the quality of judges and teams at the tournament. The result is a preference for speed, jargon, "cutting edge" argumentation, tricks, and shortcuts over substance. In truth, those elements have a place in the activity, but they should enhance substance rather than replace it.

The dangers with this hypercompetitive mindset do not end there. It also gives rise to bullying and exclusion. Early in my coaching career I judged a debate at Harvard's high school tournament in which two Black debaters who were not accustomed to speed and jargon were debating against a contemporary, national circuit team. Midway through her final speech, one of the (white) national circuit-style debaters stopped her speech. She told me she was done speaking, and she just "had to say this." She proceeded to tell me and the other team that they had no business being at the tournament if they did not know how debate was "supposed" to work. If they could not keep up and did not understand the arguments, they should not be entered in the tournament. This broke my heart, and I did not do enough to address it in the moment. It is a regret I carry with me some twenty years later.

Recently, some brave individuals started raising awareness of this toxic mentality that competitive environments can breed. In an October 2020 article, *Huffington Post* shed light on this undercurrent, interviewing "nearly a dozen former elite high school debaters who described a culture of misogyny, racism and sexual abuse—and are demanding change."[15] This, of course, is far more important than anything else in the activity. Coaches must do more to stop this abhorrent behavior. We need to work concertedly and purposefully to foster inclusivity within our teams and within the community. When we witness acts of discrimination, bullying, or worse, we cannot sit on the sidelines. We must intervene. We must correct it.

I should not have limited my response to a singular statement on the ballot alongside zero speaker points assigned to the debater when I judged that team at Harvard all those years ago. I should have stopped the round. I should have explained bluntly and immediately why her behavior was disgusting, and I should have reported the incident to the tournament staff and her coach.

Thankfully, there are signs of progress. The all-female team at the Laurel School in Ohio, coached by Rich Kawolics, is undertaking a multiyear statistical study of gender inequality in academic debate. Articles like the one in *HuffPost* are bringing attention to the issue. Ella Schnake won a national title in program oral interpretation at the high school NSDA 2019 national championship with a moving piece titled "Debate Like a Girl."[16] Within the debate space, students embracing performance-based approaches often directly address the racial, ethnic, sexual orientation, and gender inequities embedded in the activity, academia, and society.

Organizations like the Women's Debate Institute (WDI) are taking action to fix the competitive landscape. WDI seeks to provide "safe spaces, mentoring, free tuition, mobile resources and a supportive network" in order to "reverse the attrition of individuals with marginalized gender identities in the high school and college debate communities" while spreading "norms and values of intellectual integrity, kindness, compassion, and respect."[17] At the same time, the WDI and NSDA are in the early stages of working "to provide anti-harassment training specific to debate, which the institute had developed based on a Title IX training for American high school campus association."[18]

Other actors are taking broad steps as well. Individuals like Angelique Ronald, the longtime director of the California state championship tournament embraced the role of curriculum director of diversity, equity, inclusion, and justice at the Institute for Speech and Debate, where she "refocused her attention to advocating for matters of equity and inclusion in the world of speech and debate."[19] In that capacity, she "promotes solutions-based, culture-wide changes to make forensics a more accessible, open, and safe space for all."[20] As a community, we have a long way to go; however, progress is happening. Self-reflection and advancement are inherently a part of this activity.

The Solution

The solution to the problems with competitive debate begins with us, as coaches and judges. We must foster in-depth research and discussion on the arguments that are present in the debate community, in academia, and in public policy circles. While doing so, we can encourage our students to learn the theory and analysis behind a position rather than relying solely on prewritten responses drafted by other people.

Rather than rejecting the idea of speed debate, we should have students practice debating the line-by-line while signposting appropriately. Rather than punishing teams for going fast, perhaps we could teach our students to think critically and attack their opponents' arguments at the weakest link. My high school track coach, Larry Hurst, encouraged us (distance runners) to "run smarter not harder." Our debaters are certainly capable of doing the same—debating smarter not faster. Of course, a smart and fast debater is likely to beat someone who is exceptional in only one of those areas, but that is not an inherently evil thing.

Finally, we must foster a mentality within our teams that welcomes myriad viewpoints and rewards thinking that is *outside the box*. In the spirit of John Stuart Mill's marketplace of ideas, we must welcome the expression of students' differing views, if for no other reason than to ensure that students have a clearer and more complete understanding of the topics at hand. This requires us—coaches—to be educators. We have a responsibility to our students. We must do everything we can to ensure they are treated with respect and dignity.

The problem with progressive debate is not structural. It has nothing to do with talking too quickly or running generic or complex arguments.

Talking quickly helps debaters more fully develop an argument in an activity with a finite number of minutes to devote to the debate. Generic positions give them a starting point when they lack specific evidence against their opponents' arguments. The real problems at the heart of many critics' arguments against academic debate stem from overreliance on prewritten strategies, canned argumentation, sloppy line-by-line debate, and a focus on winning rather than educating. Nevertheless, we can overcome these problems through stressing the fundamentals of debate, ensuring our students partake in meaningful practice, encouraging genuine learning on the subjects we explore, and fostering a community built on respect.

Notes

1. A shorter version of this chapter appeared in the NSDA's journal, *Rostrum*, in 2010. Several prominent high school coaches had authored criticisms of the fast-paced and technical style that had flowed from the collegiate world of policy debate (NDT and CEDA) to dominate the high school's national circuit. Those trends have continued to permeate high school circuits, reaching into local and regional areas. I updated that article for inclusion in this work to account for my growing observations about trends within the debate community.

Shawn F. Briscoe, "Defending Policy Debate," *Rostrum* (February 2010): 57–61. Copyright (2010) National Speech and Debate Association. www.speechanddebate.org. Printed with permission.

2. Dan O'Rourke, "Policy Debate Is Committing Rhetorical Suicide: Let's Save Lincoln Douglas," *Rostrum* (December 2009): 17–18.

3. Bob Bilyeu, "An Army of One, A Challenge to Debate Coaches," *Rostrum* (April 2004): 82–86.

4. Here I list the various alternatives now available to high school students. At the collegiate level, we see alternative debate formats such as LD, NPDA, APDA, IPDA, BP, and PFD added to the mix.

5. Worlds-style debate also incorporates multiple disciplines simultaneously.

6. O'Rourke, 17.

7. O'Rourke, 17.

8. Shawn F. Briscoe, "Forensics: Enhancing Civic Literacy and Democracy," *Principal Leadership* (May 2009): 48.

9. O'Rourke, 17.

10. Mike Allen, Sandra Berkowitz, Steve Hunt, and Allan Louden, "Measuring the Impact of Forensics and Communication Education on Critical Thinking: A Meta-analytic Summary" (paper presented at the 83rd annual

meeting of the National Communication Association, Chicago, IL, November 19–23, 1997).

11. Briana Mezuk, Irina Bondarenko, Suzanne Smith, and Eric Tucker, "Impact of Participating in a Policy Debate Program on Academic Achievement: Evidence from the Chicago Urban Debate League," *Educational Research and Reviews* 6, no. 9 (September 5, 2011): 622–35, https://urbandebate .org/download/5/why-it-matters/335/journal-of-adolescence-mezuk-et-al.pdf.

12. Mezuk et al.

13. The NAUDL has posted several different papers written about the Chicago study. https://urbandebate.org/why-it-matters/.

14. Daniel Shackelford, "The BUDL Effect: Examining Academic Achievement and Engagement Outcomes of Preadolescent Baltimore Urban Debate League Participants" (paper for the National Association for Urban Debate Leagues, 2019), https://urbandebate.org/download/5/why-it-matters/338/the -budl-effect.pdf.

15. Emma Gray, "Competitive Debaters Are Ready for Their 'Me Too' Moment," *HuffPost*, October 1, 2020, https://www.huffpost.com/entry/high -school-debate-me-too_n_5f7217fcc5b6f622a0c2ab94 [accessed October 15, 2020].

16. National Speech and Debate Association, "Ella Schnake 'Debate Like a Girl'—Program Oral Interpretation Champion—Nationals 2019," YouTube. Online video clip, accessed October 15, 2020, https://www.youtube.com /watch?v=Ii5HtExwEDc.

17. "Mission and Story," Women's Debate Institute, no date, accessed October 15, 2020, https://womensdebateinstitute.org/.

18. Gray.

19. "Angelique Ronald," Institute for Speech and Debate, no date, accessed October 15, 2020, https://ispeechanddebate.com/faculties/angelique-ronald/.

20. "Angelique Ronald."

10.
Debate as a Framework for Business

Yari L. Mitchell

I never intended to be a debater. Entering high school, the plan was home economics. However, home economics was full, so that left Introduction to Debate as my only option for freshman elective. The most I knew about debate, at the time, was that it was done before a presidential election, and I thought those were boring. I never would have imagined that debate would become an all-consuming affair for the next decade of my life and the enduring skills it developed would be at the core of my professional success.

I participated in policy debate all four years of high school, including summer debate camps, and received scholarships to debate for the College of Eastern Utah and later the University of Miami, Florida. Today, I am chief business development officer for a start-up ophthalmic medical device company. I am a member of the executive leadership team and am responsible for the organization's global commercial launch strategy.

When I reflect on my debate and professional career together, I am struck by the similarities between these two competitive and professional arenas and how transportable the skills are from one to the other. In my experience, policy debate offers a model for how to successfully navigate the corporate environment, develop an effective value proposition, and implement an effective and dynamic business strategy. Over the following pages, I will share a few of those similarities and how I have applied my debate skills throughout my career.

Debate Is a Model for Negotiation and Business Strategy

Negotiations follow a similar format to a policy debate round. You discuss a topic, make arguments to support your position, are presented with counterarguments and/or proposals, and you need to be prepared to effectively address these rebuttals to achieve your desired result. Nearly every aspect of debate can be applied to negotiation and business strategy development. Following are just a few examples of how I applied the skills learned through my debate career to my current career in ophthalmic medical devices.

Understanding the Topic

The topic is essentially the reason you are in the room. My first year on the high school debate team the topic was *Resolved: that the United States government should significantly increase space exploration beyond Earth's mesosphere.* When a new topic was announced, the first thing I learned to do was break it down into its parts, define the key terms, and think through the word-to-word relationships. This helped establish some boundaries for the topic and a foundation from which my partner and I could develop our position, identify core arguments to make, and identify other possible policy positions to be prepared to argue against. Understanding the topic in this way is fundamental.

In the boardroom, the topics to be addressed vary greatly and have a wide range of impact on the business. Like understanding a debate topic, when developing a strategy to manage a business issue, I start with taking time to understand and define the scope of the issue. I evaluate how the issue impacts the overall business, who are the key stakeholders to be considered, what are their needs, and how might they be impacted. Once I have evaluated the players and their needs versus the business needs, next I look for possible alignments to be leveraged and conflicts that may require compromise. Taking the time to fully understand the core elements of the business issue, just like a debate topic, I have found sets me up to develop a more successful strategy and better awareness of the real issues to be addressed when I present a strategy for consideration.

Know Your Position

In a debate tournament, we must shift between arguing for and against the topic or resolution. This teaches participants how to evaluate a statement, or argument, from opposing perspectives. Arguing both for and against a topic helps identify strengths and weaknesses and taught me how to identify gaps to address or leverage depending on the situation. Understanding and leveraging strengths is the easy part. But I have found that truly understanding and confronting your weaknesses is what sets you apart from other debaters. Knowing your weaknesses in advance allows you to prepare outside of the time constraints of the debate round, so when presented with the argument in competition, you are not caught off guard and left without a response. Knowing the challenges you will face ahead of time with the argument you are putting forward and being ready to answer with strong responses mitigates the weakness and enhances your chance of winning.

This kind of critical thinking and preparation has helped me tremendously in my professional career. When building a product launch strategy, for example, I follow a similar process as I did for preparing for a debate tournament. I start by defining how my product uniquely solves a problem or addresses an unmet need. Then, I evaluate how my product stacks up against other products, what are the real or perceived weaknesses to be addressed, and what kind of challenges can I expect from my competition. And, just like in the debate season, I continuously monitor, adapt, and evolve my strategy as new information becomes available and I see how my competition reacts. While there are several tools, such as a SWOT analysis, that have been developed over the years to help commercial teams accomplish this task, my early training preparing for and competing in debate helped me establish a strong foundation and habit for strategy development, implementation, and continuous evaluation.

Identify Your Audience

Before every debate round, when postings were announced it was a mad dash to find out whom you would be competing against and who would be your judge for the round. The first thing I would do was ask my partner, teammates, coaches, and friends if they knew anything about the people in my next round. Odds were someone else knew something about my opposing team and the arguments they liked to make as well as their team strengths and weaknesses. Additionally, it was likely someone knew something about my judge and could share insights on debate styles they liked or did not like, arguments that held sway, as well as arguments that were not effective in convincing them. Understanding the players in the room helped me know what to expect and gave me just a little time to prepare for the round more effectively.

In my professional career, the same is true. The first thing I want to know when going to any meeting is who will be in the room. I want to know what their interests and/or organization goals are, do they have any biases, and what is their history on the topic to be discussed. While seemingly not as important as the topic, understanding the players makes a big difference between getting the budget you need versus the budget that is left over. In my career, I have worked for small, mid-sized, and large companies. Regardless of the corporate structure, there is always an annual budget negotiation. To secure my budget I present a detailed strategy that demonstrates how my initiatives align with the company goals and objectives. However, even the best laid plans do not always get funded. This is why I endeavor to find out who the decision-makers are, what kind of initiatives resonate and what don't, what kind of arguments are effective in a budget negotiation with these individuals, and what are other teams offering for plans and requesting budget-wise. While asking for scoop on competitive debate teams and presiding judges is a small thing in the grand scheme of debate, I found it to be a good habit that served me well professionally.

Investigate the Source!

Knowing the source of a claim is more important now than ever. In a debate round, I would often challenge an opposing team's source, or evidence, for a claim, and with good reason. Not all sources are created equal. The foundation of a strong argument is the evidence to support the claim and the connection of a claim to other claims. Without evidentiary support for a claim, the validity is impossible to determine. If a core claim of an argument is unsubstantiated by sufficient evidence, it is likely the whole argument will fail. The consequences in debate can be as small as winning an argument or as great as winning a tournament.

In the real-world, lack of evidence to support a claim can mean the difference between making a sale, getting your company funded, getting a medical device approved by the FDA, and it can even be the difference between life and death. The kind of argument you make will dictate the kind of source you need (i.e. do you need a physician or an economist), the quality of the source (i.e. do they need credentials or not, are the findings supported or contradicted by others), and the quantity of sources you need (i.e. is a single-source generally accepted or do you need multiple sources) to support your argument.

When developing a competitive strategy for my sales team, I always look at what the competition is saying and what evidence they use to support their claims. While a case report is informative on the potential of a product but not conclusive, a prospective, controlled, randomized study of several hundred people is significantly more reliable. Further, who the source is matters. If an employee of the company makes a positive report it may be reliable, but it may also be heavily biased. Multiple independent sources reporting results from a large number of study participants are generally more reliable. Understanding the quality, quantity, and level of potential bias in a source can help you determine if the claim has merit and needs to be countered or if it is unreliable and not worth addressing in your sales strategy.

Learn. Adapt. Repeat.

Over the course of a debate season, teams hone their strategies and arguments taking advantage of lessons learned from debate tournaments, team members, news media, and newly published literature. To stay ahead, advance your position, and increase the number of wins over the course of the year, it is critical to keep up with changes from your competitors and integrate new arguments and evidence.

I found the same to be true in a corporate environment. In my industry of ophthalmic medical devices, my competitors are constantly evolving their messaging, launching new products, and acquiring companies. To create space in a crowded channel I need to follow my competitors closely and listen for changes. I am critical of their sources and my own and am constantly looking for ways to bolster my position and new ways to counter my competition. Most importantly, I pay attention to what does not work and adjust accordingly. Developing and implementing a business strategy is an iterative process. Just like a debate tournament and season, the players change, the arguments evolve, and new evidence becomes available. Staying on top of these dynamics is vital to achieving and maintaining your desired results.

The Persistent Value of Debate

I believe ending up in the Introduction to Debate class my freshman year in high school drastically changed the course of my career in a positive way. Aside from the enduring friendships, the opportunity to learn about social, economic, environmental, and political issues was invaluable. Getting to construct and debate policy ideas and understand connectedness between policy decisions and public impact from an early age helped me become a better critical thinker, strategist, and communicator. Out of everything I learned in school, I use the knowledge and skills garnered from debate every day. No other program, or course, can match the profound and meaningful impact debate has had on my professional success.

11.
Engaging Each Other on the Merits of Our Arguments

Sean Luechtefeld

There's no debate over whether the United States is experiencing a time of heightened polarization. But what's driving that polarization? In political circles, Republicans blame Democrats while Democrats blame Republicans. Pollsters might point to demographic differences, finding evidence of growing divides between urban and rural voters or highly educated voters versus those with only a high school diploma. Still others might insist social media, by enabling us to create our own little echo chambers, is driving America apart.

While I won't deny these factors are playing into polarization, I argue that we ought to pay more attention to a broader factor: we have lost sight of how to engage with one other in arguments. Whether at the Thanksgiving dinner table or in the comments on your Facebook News Feed, even minor disagreements can trigger a volcanic eruption that spews vitriol everywhere. We've all seen it, and most of us have been guilty of it ourselves. We react to something someone said without listening to the merits of their argument. We comment on an article we see on social media after having read only the headline. We insist we know we're right, only to realize that we misunderstood some important piece of information.

On the other hand, we find that conversations—even when we strongly disagree with our interlocutors—are much more productive when all parties take a step back, listen, consider the evidence presented, and approach one another on the merits of the claims being made. These are the same skills cultivated by participation in competitive debate.

Inspired by my older sister/role model, Lyn, who was on the high school debate team, I spent four years competing in Lincoln-Douglas debate at Fort Walton Beach High School, and later went on to compete in policy debate at Florida State University. That paved the way for me to coach policy debate at Wake Forest University, where I earned my master's degree in communication. Together, the nine years I spent in competitive debate helped me see how debate cultivates a set of skills, which I believe have the power to make people more adept at engaging with one another.

Our social discourse would be far less heated and far less polarizing if everyone had the opportunity to develop four competencies fostered by debate: the ability to disentangle claims, the ability to marshal and critique evidence, the ability to adapt to audiences, and the ability to see the complex ways seemingly unrelated issues are connected. In this chapter, I highlight the importance of these skills by drawing on my own personal experiences—experiences that have been made possible in large part by my participation in debate. These experiences include earning a PhD; spending fifteen years communicating on behalf of mission-driven organizations working to advance racial wealth equity, the civil rights of people with disabilities and more; and preparing professionals to excel in communications careers as an adjunct professor in the master's program in communication at Johns Hopkins University.

Disentangling Claims

In 1999, the U.S. Supreme Court gave power to the Americans with Disabilities Act (ADA) by issuing its landmark decision in *Olmstead v. LC.* The plaintiffs in the case were two women living in a state-run institution for people with mental illness and intellectual disabilities, and the women were forced to remain institutionalized despite professional assessments confirming they were capable of and could benefit from living independently in the community. In the lower courts, the state of Georgia argued that enabling the plaintiffs to transition to independent living would disrupt funding streams and could lead to closures of the state's mental health hospitals.

Ultimately, the Supreme Court ruled 6–3 in favor of the plaintiffs, with Justice Ruth Bader Ginsberg authoring the Court's majority opinion. The Court's decision, Ginsberg wrote, reflected two evident judgments: that institutionalizing people who can benefit from community integration "perpetuates unwarranted assumptions" that people so isolated are unworthy of community life; and that "confinement in an institution severely diminishes the everyday life activities" of the people so confined.

Crucial to the significant civil rights victory made possible by the *Olmstead* decision was the ability of those arguing the case to disentangle two distinct claims, one about funding for mental hospitals and the other about the civil rights of people with disabilities. The state of Georgia may very well have been correct about its assessments of the impact of complying with the ADA on state funding, but the skilled debaters who argued on behalf of the plaintiffs understood that those concerns were secondary to the question of whether forced institutionalization violated the rights enumerated by the ADA. These arguers knew that if they could prove the state was violating the plaintiff's civil rights, concerns about funding for institutions were irrelevant.

The skill exhibited by those who argued the *Olmstead* case is the same skill fostered by participation in competitive debate. The ability to listen to the merits of a case, disentangle the various claims being made, build a counterposition that focuses on only the most relevant issues, and prioritize key arguments are all central to debate education. In competitive policy debate, for example, debaters learn that it isn't sufficient to have a plan with a couple of advantages, nor is it adequate to introduce a counterplan that solves for the other team's plan. Rather, the advantages of the plan must outweigh its disadvantages, while a proposed counterplan must be net beneficial compared to the plan.

Marshaling and Critiquing Evidence

Another essential competency fostered by debate has to do with finding, analyzing, and leveraging evidence. As I write this chapter, the COVID-19 pandemic continues raging in the United States. Whereas several countries have successfully slowed the spread of the deadly virus and at least one (New Zealand) has eradicated it, the U.S. is now responsible for more than a quarter of the 105 million-plus cases confirmed worldwide. A range of factors explain our country's poor response to the pandemic, including inaction by the federal government to support local health authorities, Americans' unwillingness to quarantine, Americans' unwillingness to wear masks, skepticism surrounding vaccines, and more. Because the pandemic continues its unrelenting rage, ensuring people with disabilities are prioritized for receiving the vaccine is a key focus of the work my colleagues and I are doing at ANCOR, a nonprofit trade association whose 1,600+ members deliver critical services to people with intellectual and developmental disabilities.

Although each of the factors hastening the spread of COVID-19 in the United States plays out in different ways, they share one thing in common: adherence to something other than the best available evidence. Consider, for example, a common retort offered by opponents of mask mandates: *We know X* (X could be "masks are uncomfortable" or "it's my right not to wear a mask"), *but there's no evidence that masks actually do anything to keep us safe.*" Quite the contrary, there is abundant evidence that masks, when worn properly, are effective in preventing the spread of COVID-19, especially when indoors or when social distancing is impossible. A more accurate statement is that people do not care to access evidence about the effectiveness of masking, or they do not know how to, or they do not know how to make sense of the evidence they can access.

Across more than a decade of teaching, I have found that this ability to marshal evidence—and critique evidence presented by others—is one skill among many that sets my students with debate experience apart from their peers. Debate teaches students how to research to find evidence, how to effectively craft warrants that connect evidence to claims, how to make comparisons between different types of evidence presented, and how to identify when evidence should not be considered credible. These competencies mean that while students without debate experience often make claims *and then* search for whatever source they can find to support those claims, students with debate experience are able to synthesize broad bodies of information *first*, and then craft claims accordingly.

Adapting to Audiences

In 2017, before I joined the staff, ANCOR spent the better part of the summer fighting to protect the Medicaid program as Republican lawmakers attempted to repeal the Affordable Care Act (ACA). ACA proponents fully expected it would be repealed because Republicans controlled both chambers of Congress and the White House. In May of that year, the House voted

217–213 in favor of the repeal, sending the bill to the Senate. After two months of sharp public debate about health care during which tens of thousands of advocates jammed the Capitol switchboards, flooded senators' email inboxes, and rallied on the National Mall, the Senate ultimately voted in late July against the measure in a 49–51 vote. Those who assumed the Senate would vote purely on party lines were surprised when three Republican senators joined Democratic senators in voting against the repeal: John McCain of Arizona, Susan Collins of Maine, and Lisa Murkowski of Alaska.

Those three leaders, though necessary, were insufficient for preserving the ACA. In addition, protecting the ACA required the tens of thousands of advocates sounding a consistent message that could sway the votes of the three moderate Republican Senators. Those advocates understood that political party is not the only factor that motivates lawmakers' votes, and that to be successful, they needed to understand which other factors could motivate Senators Murkowski, McCain, and Collins, and needed to tailor their pro-ACA message to those motivations in a way that remained consistent with the messages being conveyed to the other ninety-seven senators.

These are essential skills that participation in competitive debate cultivates. As debaters, students learn that different judges have different preferences regarding depth of argument, quantity of evidence, willingness to consider procedural arguments, openness to critiques of conventional modes of debate, and more. As students learn these different preferences, they also learn to adapt. In my first year at Florida State University, for example, my debate partner, Kimmy, and I had three different versions of our affirmative case, which aimed to reduce fossil fuel consumption by investing in organic farming. Which case we presented largely depended on the judge we were assigned in each debate. Running all three cases over the course of the season enabled us to become educated about a wider range of issues and adept at defending a more diverse range of claims.

Understanding the Complexity of Interrelated Issues

My doctoral research examined how a group of unemployed workers who became known as Coxey's Army crafted arguments to justify two seemingly unrelated claims: that federal economic policy should aim to create jobs, and that people have the right to protest in public spaces in our nation's capital. Understood by historians as the first-ever march on Washington, Coxey's Army marched from Ohio to D.C. in 1894 to petition the federal government for what today would be considered an economic stimulus package. The challenge Jacob Coxey and his "petition in boots" faced was that there was no precedent for the federal government to pass economic policies that were designed to help individuals—until that point, economic policymaking was largely confined to the macroeconomic arena. To illustrate the need for congressional action, Coxey's Army planned to stage a grand demonstration at the east front of the U.S. Capitol. However, this approach further complicated their mission, as they also lacked precedent for using public spaces in our nation's capital for public demonstrations. In response, Coxey's Army crafted a unified argument that insisted on two rights: the right of every willing person to work *and* the right of the people to take their grievances directly to the seat of their government when their other rights were jeopardized.

I suspect Jacob Coxey and his followers did not have competitive debate experience, but the skill they exhibited in crafting a single argument to effectively address seemingly disjointed issues illustrates their mastery of a skill that is central to debate education. Public discourse tends to cast issues in one-dimensional terms, even though nearly all major questions with which society grapples are much more complex. When it comes to abortion, for example, we often talk about the right to life or the right to choose; we rarely talk about the economic conditions that might lead someone to consider terminating her pregnancy. When it comes to racial wealth disparities, we often talk about the value of hard work; we rarely discuss policies and structures that have historically made it harder for Black families to build wealth. And when it comes to disaster response, we often talk about how much the federal government should spend on relief; we rarely talk about the underlying climate conditions that are causing things like hurricanes and wildfires to be more frequent and more intense.

By participating in debate, students learn the myriad ways that issues relate to one another, and that how we frame issues brings certain aspects into focus while obscuring others. Students with debate experience know that the abortion debate *is* about rights, but it is *also* about what our society should do to support families. Students with debate experience know that building wealth *is* about hard work, but it is *also* about the extent to which public policy enables people to pursue higher education or buy a home. Students with debate experience understand that disaster response *is* about government spending, but it is *also* about climate change. Debating teaches us that none of the questions with which we grapple are *either/or*—they are always *both/and*.

Far from the stereotypes I faced in high school and college, debaters do not just argue for the sake of arguing (*most of the time, anyway*), nor do we default to an argumentative stance in every interaction we have. Rather, we debate because we know that debating isn't about combat—it's about critical thinking. It's about considering social problems, testing ideas, and comparing and contrasting an available set of solutions. Our debates are most productive when we engage one another by listening, considering the merits of the claims presented, and recognizing that disagreement doesn't have to be disorderly. I honestly believe that if everyone had the opportunity to develop these competencies through participation in debate, our social discourse would be far less divisive—our society far less polarized.

Just imagine if everyone in our country spent just two years honing the skills fostered through competitive debate. What would it mean if that relative at your Thanksgiving dinner table didn't immediately resort to demonizing Republicans at the first mention of an idea popular among Democrats, or vice versa? What would it mean if people stopped posting mean comments on your Facebook post because they read the headline of the article you shared but didn't actually click on it? What would it mean if you felt confident that your member of Congress is just as motivated by her constituents' needs as she is by her party's leadership?

How we get there from here remains unclear, and just because I enjoyed the benefit of debate doesn't mean I have all the answers. But thanks to my time in debate, I know the skills I developed can help me be part of the solution.

12.
A Mother's Journey from Debate to the NICU

Tara L. Tate

I believe individuals throw around the term "life-changing" in ways that somewhat strip the term of its meaning. The term should only be used for those truly significant events, like a marriage, a death of someone close, or change in career. The term should also be reserved for a consistent series of choices one makes over time that changes who they fundamentally are as a person. To say that debate, for me, was not only *life-changing* but potentially *life-saving* comes with knowing how impactful and meaningful those words can be.

I always knew debate helped shape who I was. I don't remember much of my life that was absent of debate. My mother was my high school debate coach. My father was a college professor of social studies. I grew up in a household that was articulate, socially aware, and opinionated. Debate was a natural attraction to me in high school because it is what I knew. I grew up at tournaments watching my mom pencil in scores in a tabroom and timekeeping rounds as soon as I could understand the workings of a stopwatch. I knew early in life that I did not have much physical talent, prowess, or strength. But the use of my words and wit? That was a different story.

Debate is what paid for a good portion of my undergraduate career through scholarship money, even transferring universities so I could increase my debate opportunities. Debate paid my way through my master's program as a graduate assistant, and I left academia with minimal loans. It formulated my friendship circle. It is where I often found my romantic interests. The community of debate individuals that I knew, enjoyed, and loved had for, most of my adult life, been my primary draw as to why I stayed in the community. In essence, it was a second home for me.

Although I always knew the portable skills that debate brought to its participants, it was hard for me to truly understand that praxis since I taught debate. I could easily explain to students the various skills they would develop through debate and how that would transfer to life outside our activity, such as work and relationships. For me, I could not personally feel the impact since I was using debate skills to teach debate. I always felt I was effective at convincing my debate students how important the skills were that they were learning. My life had, for the most part, been mostly using my debate skills to persuade others about the importance of debate. At least professionally, I was not transferring those skills to outside arenas. It was not until I was winding down my career as an active national circuit high school debate director and facing a personal trauma that I started seeing how debate provided me an arsenal of weapons to use in a situation that was not merely life-changing, but life-saving.

To understand what I mean by that, it might be necessary to look a little further back in time. Debate can be all consuming—and for me it was. My late twenties and thirties went by in a blink of an eye as I was flying high school students all over the country weekend after weekend for them to compete at the highest levels of competition. I knew I always wanted a family, but I was very happy and fulfilled with what my debate life brought to me, even though it likely meant I was not giving proper focus to my personal life. There was always one more class of students that I just needed to see through to the finish line or one more competitive goal I just had not reached with my students that kept me coming back. Life eventually led me to the man I was to marry in my late thirties, and we knew it was time to start focusing on creating a family. Certainly, many individuals balance debate coaching and a family. For me, however, I tend to jump all in when given a focus. I knew that, for me, I could not remain at the competitive level I was at coaching debate and be a good mother and partner to my husband.

I got pregnant at thirty-nine years of age and informed my school district that I was not returning to direct the program the following year. During my pregnancy, I kept up most of my travel and active coaching duties. Other than a scary bout of food poisoning early on, I was able to be an effective debate coach and maintain due diligence to a healthy pregnancy. By all accounts, I had a rockstar pregnancy until twenty-nine weeks along in what should have been a thirty-nine-week pregnancy.

It was a Friday in March, and I was scheduled for an appointment with my OB-GYN that morning. Since I was later in age during my pregnancy, my OB-GYN was actually a team of nine specialists who focused on geriatric pregnancies. Everyone had been impressed that my pregnancy had zero hiccups through the first two trimesters and the early part of the third. My husband and I drove separate cars to the appointment that morning. We were excited to see our little peanut on the screen and both of us were going to work after the appointment. I had my overnight bag in the back of my car since I was traveling with my students to our National Speech and Debate Association national qualifying debate tournament later that afternoon.

After being with the nurse for a few minutes, it was clear something was wrong. My blood pressure was sky-high. My protein levels in my urine sample were over double what they should have been. The doctor was explaining what "preeclampsia with severe features" meant to me and my husband. Instead of walking out to go to our cars, I was wheeled down to Labor and Delivery despite only being twenty-nine weeks/five days along in my pregnancy. My OB-GYN told me that the hope was that they could get my blood pressure down but there was a chance I was going to deliver that day. Although our peanut was not ready to leave my body, my body had become too toxic for me to continue to house her safely. Each additional day that I was pregnant, I was risking extremely high blood pressure and damage to my liver and kidneys. The possibility of a stroke was very much in the conversation. Preeclampsia also means there is restricted blood flow to the placenta, meaning our baby's life was also at risk. Every additional day put us both in danger.

We were able to extend my pregnancy thirteen more days. Then, my body told me, "No more." We delivered our child via cesarean section at thirty-one weeks/four days into my pregnancy. She weighed a precious yet terrifying three pounds and eight ounces. Here was this perfectly formed human but in the tiniest of packages. My husband was able to cut the umbilical cord and I was able to lay my eyes on her for a few precious seconds. My heart filled with love immediately. She was immediately whisked away to the Infant Specialty Care Unit of the hospital, otherwise known as the Neonatal Intensive Care Unit (NICU).

In the days before I delivered, I was told we were not going to be able to carry my baby to full-term. My husband and I were given a tour of the NICU and told about the many possible complications. We were told that most babies go home around the time of their original due date. For us, we were told to estimate being in the NICU for four to six weeks. That amount of time seemed agonizing and impossible at the onset. Little did we know that we would experience a stay that was nearly four times that length. Our NICU stay was initially 129 days at two different hospitals. My baby needed escalated care that the hospital where we had been for four weeks could not provide, so she was transferred to a large children's hospital an hour away from home. Then, she tacked on another fourteen-day NICU stay after her second abdomen surgery when she was six months old.

Despite the psychological tunnel that a NICU stay has on a parent, I was cognizant very early on about some of the surface-level advantages that debate had given me. It was debate, and solely debate, that years prior had landed me at a north Chicagoland public high school that paid its teachers very well, both regarding salary and health benefits. It was clear early on that my school-provided insurance meant our hospital bill would be zero, despite having a $1.5 million NICU baby when everything was said and done. It was so many debate friends and colleagues that created a comfort of support for me through social media as I started to share our daily struggle in the hospital. Former debate partners quickly reached out to my family to ask if crowdsource funding pages were needed. My debate family surrounded me with support, advice, and love.

It was not until the darkest days were behind us that I truly started seeing how debate was a huge factor at my baby's bedside. My daughter was not just a preemie facing normal struggles. She had developed necrotizing enterocolitis, an infection in the bowel that can cause the bowel to die off. Her infection had become surgical when her bowel perforated. Her experienced surgeon said it was one of the most difficult surgeries he had ever done; he thought for the first hour after opening her up that he was likely just going to have to close her back up. During her darkest days, a chaplain visited her isolette on four different occasions because it was not known if she would live to see the morning. I absolutely credit my daughter's outstanding surgeon, her knowledgeable attending doctors, and her superpower-possessing nurses with her survival. However, study after study done of infants in the NICU will tell you that parental involvement is also an important factor in a baby's survival. I did not realize how much my involvement relied on the portable skills that debate had taught me in order to be the parent my newborn needed. All the skills I had been teaching my students for so many years, such as quality research, resilience, and cost-benefit analysis decision-making, were now front and center in my NICU-focused life.

The most important debate skill that quickly became relevant, even in the early days of my diagnosis and before our child arrived, was the importance of quality *research*. Even in the days prior to her arrival, my time on hospital bedrest was spent reading everything I could get my hands on about preeclampsia, NICU practices, and premature babies. I immediately had to start weeding out the websites that were not backed by medical expertise or those that unnecessarily fed my anxiety. The internet can be an unlimiting rabbit hole of sources, so my ability to process and organize the various pieces of information was important. Just like a debate article can branch off to give you five more leads on ways you can spin your argument, every article I found on my current medical crisis led me to numerous more questions and ideas I wanted to research. Although I did not quite start cutting cards about my medical crisis, I did take notes and organize my internet investigation in the same format I would have if I were starting the research process of a new debate argument. It was automatic. The ability to organize and categorize the overwhelming amount of research was so important in regard to being well-grounded when our daughter was born but it also was instrumental in the days following her birth.

On Day 7 of my daughter's life, I had snuck out of my constant NICU vigil for two hours because my cat was also facing a medical emergency. As I was driving back to the hospital, my cell phone rang. I looked down at the phone and the caller ID read NICU. I immediately pulled over because a call from the NICU is rarely good news. It was the head of neonatology asking me if I was returning soon. I was able to get back to the NICU in about ten minutes and was met by a team of doctors and nurses. This was the day I was told my child had necrotizing enterocolitis (NEC). What followed was a lot of complex medical terminology that I did not understand about what this condition was. Fortunately, as the neonatologist started explaining, I grabbed the legal pad and pen that I had been keeping in the bottom shelf underneath the isolette. (*I kid you not. I had a legal pad stored there to take notes during the doctors' rounds and jot down questions that came up when a doctor was not specifically attending to us.*) I started essentially flowing all the information the medical team was giving me. I wanted as close to exact wording as possible. As the neonatologist wrapped up his discussion with me, his final piece of advice was, "It is best for you to stay off the internet. If you have questions, please ask one of us." My mother, husband, and I were then led to a private family room so we could process the information.

Stay off the internet? Who was he kidding? When we got in the private family room, I immediately took out my cell phone and googled the phrase "necrotizing enterocolitis and death." After about thirty seconds of scanning article titles and summaries, I fell to my knees and my phone fell to the ground. I don't ever recall a time in my life where I lost all feeling and strength to stand like I did in that moment. That moment is still one of the most vivid I have from this time six years ago. After some time sobbing and screaming (and being comforted by my husband and mother), I got myself to the couch, took a deep breath, and the debater inside of me took over. What had I expected with a search string like that?

I knew I needed all the information, but I needed to focus on more scientific and productive articles that would provide me the information I needed to advocate for my daughter. I needed scholarly articles but ones that I could understand as a layperson. I quickly went to a clean page on my legal pad and started writing search strings that included words like symptoms, parental support, and recovery. It allowed me to productively research the deadly infection that my premature baby had contracted that was now causing her bowel to die off. I needed to hear the information about how serious it was but the sharp research tools that debate gave me allowed me to find the articles that were the most relevant to me. The neonatologist had explained that NEC became life-threatening when the bowel basically ruptured and surgical intervention was required. I started developing a long list of symptoms of surgical NEC on my legal pad.

As a parent of a NICU baby, you rely on the doctors and nurses for their medical expertise. However, they rely on you knowing the slightest changes in your baby as you sit vigil at their bedside. Although the doctors and nurses were observing, I needed to know whether or not her belly was turning gray. Did it appear distended? Was she appearing lethargic? Was I sensing that she was feeling more pain? Those questions were vital over the next few days as the NEC continued to deaden her bowel, and she was rushed into surgery for a procedure that her rockstar surgeon says was one of the most complicated he had ever had to perform.

Linked to the need for quality research is the importance of asking the necessary questions when you are in this type of medical crisis. Although it may be a rather shallow analogy, some of the questioning periods I had with Kelcie's medical team were some of the most intimidating *cross-examinations* I have ever been in. It is hard to be a layperson asking the hard questions of medical personnel, some of which did not have the most nurturing bedside manner. I also had to shed some of my autopilot debate beliefs. I had to admit when I did not understand and then ask the question. I had to ask questions often where I did not already know the answer. However, debate teaches you to be like a dog with a bone. You keep asking the question until you get a satisfying answer. I always teach my novice competitors that a good cross-examination is when you have two to three questions prepared but the rest of the time is built on asking probing questions from the answers you are given.

The medical personnel certainly were not my "opponents" but the ability to quickly ask follow-up question after follow-up question was important. Numerous specialists would come by Kelcie's isolette during rounds, but it was often for a brief period. I had to quickly and efficiently use that small window of time they gave me to ask questions (often it did seem like they were giving me the three minutes).[1] There were often a few times where I just sensed something was off and I had to question a call made by someone with a lot more medical expertise than I. I would not necessarily say this was mother's intuition, but I was the one that was observing my baby's habits most acutely. It is not easy asking *why* a procedure or a treatment is being done but debate skills give one the confidence to ask the hard questions.

One of the primary decision-making tools a debater learns is that of *cost-benefit analysis.* Most arguments advanced in a competitive policy debate round involve weighing the benefits of a decision with the costs also involved. It is rare that a solution offered in a debate round is either 100 percent advantageous or disadvantageous; a judge often decides whether the solution yields more good than harm. One of the toughest parts one must wrap their head around in the NICU is that the solution for one medical crisis often leads to another one. For example, there was a period of time that Kelcie was on an oscillating ventilator. This is a ventilator that is much more intense than what we commonly think of. It provides significantly more oxygen, and the equipment gently vibrates the baby consistently as it works to get oxygen to every facet of her lungs. Although this type of ventilator was necessary to save her life, high amounts of oxygen for a newborn can cause blindness. Kelcie was on a consistent regimen of antibodies to fight off certain infections, but they were also causing good fungal-fighting agents to die off. Caffeine is often administered to premature babies that are having issues breathing on their own. However, too much can cause rapid heart rate on an organ that is not strong enough to handle it. When her doctors and specialists would complete rounds by her bedside each day, the conversations were very much set up in this cost-benefit analysis approach. Which is the most acute and life-threatening problem the baby is currently facing? How do the treatments and procedures to improve one crisis affect other health problems she is facing? When do we stop a treatment because the risks of continuing it now outweigh benefits moving forward?

A debate round is a complex interplay of a lot of different arguments to arrive at a final conclusion, and the treatment of the myriad of health crises of a sick, premature baby operates in the same way. Without that debate training of processing costs and benefits of a decision, as well as the interplay between arguments, I am not sure I would have adequately processed the vast number of medical decisions in a way that was effective. In so many instances, it allowed me to understand why the medical specialists were prioritizing a certain treatment despite risks it may cause in other areas. Being able to quickly understand and get on board with the myriad of decisions being made by experts on behalf of my baby allowed me to be an effective teammate in her medical care. In most instances, I did not need continued reassurance that the right call was being made despite the risks. My brain, because of debate, had been programmed to process that important decisions often inherently come with risk.

In the 129 days during my daughter's first NICU stay (she returned a few months later for a follow-up surgery), there was rarely a day that I was not at her bedside morning until night. This was true even when she was transferred to a hospital an hour away because her care needed to be elevated. My husband often equated my daily journey to the NICU as a "punch in the gut" over and over again. A good day in the NICU is never the emotional equivalent to a bad day. A good day may mean that she took ten cc's of formula from a bottle. A bad day meant that a chaplain was praying over her isolette because we did not know if she would survive until morning. It is quite common to refer to a long-term NICU experience as a roller coaster because there are so many ups and downs. You must rebound from bad news fast.

Debate taught me that type of quick *resilience*. Very few competitive activities teach you how to quickly rebound after a setback the way competitive debate does. If you have a tough loss in a football game or a tennis match, you typically have some time to recover and learn from your mistakes. In debate, you must learn and rebound from a hard loss in real time. Your next debate could be starting within an hour. During our time in the NICU, it became a common routine for me after hearing about a setback Kelcie was facing to go find a quiet space in the hospital for about ten minutes. During that time, I would work through my emotions but also start making a plan of action for when I entered back through the double doors of the NICU. Debate taught me how to process bad news quickly and efficiently. It taught me how to handle setbacks and let downs in a way that I could quickly do better next time.

I spent the first four months of Kelcie's life at the side of her isolette morning, noon, and night. I was there for as long as I could stay awake and stay focused. I was next to her as long as my physical body and mind could endure. To be honest, my vigilance at her side was primarily due to just not knowing what else I was supposed to do. I was a new mother. My baby was at the hospital. I only knew that I was supposed to be with her. It was not until I was in therapy months after my daughter was safely home that I started to unpackage how I had mentally survived this trauma. It was not until those conversations started unraveling that I became acutely aware of how the skills I learned in debate allowed me to mentally survive the gauntlet of trauma I experienced every day she was in the hospital.

I shared some of these thoughts with other "debate parents" who went through similar NICU experiences and that knowledge of how debate shaped our experiences and effectiveness during that time only continued to expand. It was through those conversations and reflections that I realized debate allowed me to be a mother that could advocate for her child in the midst of the most complicated medical issues. It was debate that allowed me to research and understand the next crisis we were dealing with effectively and quickly. It was debate that gave me the confidence to ask the necessary questions. It was debate that allowed me to process all the information about benefits and risks of each medical decision that was made on behalf of my child's life. It was debate that gave me the resilience to be the best parent

I could be for my child, which was as important as the medicine she was receiving through her IVs.

Do I think debate saved my baby's life? I reserve most of that credit to the amazing doctors and nurses that were the expert hands, minds, and hearts that led us through this crisis. However, there is no doubt that the entire experience of our 129 days in the NICU was profoundly impacted by the training that debate provided me. As I look at my healthy six-year-old riding past me on her indoor scooter as I type this, I cannot allow myself to even think how life would be different for us without the skills debate taught me. Dare I say it would have been life-changing without them.

Notes

1. *Editor's note*: three minutes is the standard length of time allowed for cross-examination in policy debate.

Interlude
Classrooms of Compassion

Shawn F. Briscoe

> Difference is that raw and powerful connection from
> which our personal power is forged . . . We have been
> taught to either ignore our differences or to view them
> as causes for separation and suspicion rather than as
> forces for change. Without community, there is no liber-
> ation . . . Survival is learning to take our difference and
> make them strengths.
>
> > Audre Lorde, "The Master's Tools Will
> > Never Dismantle the Master's House"

Talk to me for more than a few minutes, and you learn I am passionate
about this activity called speech and debate. More than thirty years
ago I was introduced to the traditional, audience-friendly circuit of
rural Missouri. Within two months, I was hooked and immersed
myself in the activity over the next four years. When I went to college,
I dove into the contemporary, faced-paced and jargon-filled world of
debate as a member of the United States Air Force Academy policy

debate team. There, I fell in love with policy. Over those eight years spent competing in high school and college, the activity shaped me into the person I am today. After serving in the United States Air Force, I changed careers to become an educator and coach.

A few years ago, I contemplated a new job that would prevent me from working with students in speech and debate. As I wrestled with that decision, I discussed it with a colleague in Saint Louis. He advised that I might not be happy in that role because (in his words) debate was part of my identity. For better or worse, this truth means I am passionate about academic debate. This passion has had both positive and negative effects on my life and my thoughts about changes within the community.

For instance, when I first confronted nontraditional or *performance debate*, I felt personally attacked. How could something I care so deeply about be changed? I disparaged the practice, wrote it off as less than genuine, and argued that it damaged the activity. Thankfully, I am an educator first, and this activity is transformative by nature. At a tournament hosted by the University of Nevada, Las Vegas, two debaters challenged my preconceived notion of *performance debate*. Over the course of a single debate round and a bidirectional postround critique, the very debaters I was assigned to judge educated me. This should not come as a surprise.

In our teacher preparation programs, we are taught that students have different learning styles and that we should adapt our teaching to accommodate the needs of our students. We spend time exploring what it means to foster inclusive learning spaces. I believe in those principles wholeheartedly. Yet, as a coach, I apparently had blinders. I was limited by my passion for an activity that shaped my identity. I was troubled by the alternative approaches and in some cases outright attacks on the form of the activity that I knew to be transforming and empowering. I felt the power of the activity upon my life every day. I saw the positive influence of the activity on my students, alumni, and colleagues every day. To see the attacks levied by *performance debaters* on something I held so close to me was painful.

And now . . .

To think that people like myself looked down upon students who dared to express their identity in this space. Some people go further, telling those students that who they are, the way they communicate, and the way they see the world is devoid of merit, illegitimate, unwanted. How could we? *How could I?*

Yes. This is a competitive activity with norms, conventions, and rules that shape how the participants conduct themselves. But, before that, it is an academic activity, and we are educators who have a responsibility to students. To hear them. To see them. To accept them.

I have been blessed with many outstanding teachers in my life, several of whom have been mentioned elsewhere in this text. During my graduate degree work, I encountered amazing professors who shared important lessons that all educators should carry with them as they design their classrooms and interact with students. Our students come from diverse backgrounds with different codes, dialects, and communication patterns. The diverse populations that make up our communities have different ways of being and knowing. The best educators build a community of learners.

Codes, Dialects, and Communication Patterns

"The final product of our training must be neither a psychologist nor a brickmason, but a man."[1] These words, written by W.E.B. Du Bois in 1903 speak of the ideal aspiration teachers hold. In any circumstance, the path is difficult. When a cultural divide separates student from teacher, the task becomes even more challenging. The key to bridging the gap lies in effective communication. Professor of human relations at the University of Oklahoma, George Henderson, underscored this point indicating, "Where there is an inability to adequately communicate, a sense of isolation results."[2] As an educator and coach, these thoughts have profound meaning. My goal should not be to make debaters, but citizens—to help students grow into responsible human beings. In pursuit of that goal, I must open myself to my students.

Henderson explained that "the preponderance of research indicates few colleges of education are adequately preparing teachers for cultural diversity," and that "while most of the white teachers want to develop positive relations with black students, they do not succeed."[3] Throughout his course and texts, he discussed several of the reasons for this divide. While there is obviously not a panacea for resolving differences in communication, one of his central points was that white teachers simply do not understand the experiences of their Black students, nor do they accept differences in communication styles.

He explained that "some black students are extremely defensive in class with white teachers, and those who behave this way are usually merely protecting their egos."[4] Thus, in many instances in which confrontations occur between a white teacher and Black students, the students are merely protecting themselves by asserting their presence. Teachers, in turn, perceive this as a challenge to their authority, creating a vicious cycle of negative interactions, which ultimately end in disciplinary action and/or emotional or physical withdrawal by the student.

In addition, Henderson spoke of differences in language and posture across cultures. Two friends could be having a conversation in the doorway or hallway before class. White teachers often mistake their word choices, intonation, and posture as hostile even though it may be nothing of the sort. Again, these students are often sent to the principal's office for fighting. The students are baffled, resentful, or angry at the teacher because they have once again gotten in trouble for doing nothing wrong.

Sadly, this begins at an absurdly young age. Furthermore, we cannot write it off as something that only happened in the past. It does, in fact, persist: "In 2016, research from the Yale Child Study Center determined that, as early as preschool, educators tend to police Black students' responses to their authority. They perceive Black students as exhibiting more 'challenging behavior'—including 'willful defiance,' 'insubordination' and 'disrespect'—than their non-Black peers."[5]

Similarly, many educators become defensive when students converse with one another in a language other than English. Across our country, it is not uncommon for teachers to directly or indirectly deny their students the freedom to converse in their native tongues in the classroom.[6] Take two Spanish-speaking students, for example. How often are they discouraged or denied the opportunity to speak in their primary language? Never mind that doing so may be more efficient and more enlightening when discussing the content of the day. Never mind that a quick exchange in a native tongue may provide respite, connection, and release from an otherwise stressful day.

At best, we rob these students of a unique opportunity for growth as they explore our lessons with the benefits afforded from multilingual or multicultural exploration. At worst, we strip them of their identity, denying them the right to their own sense of self and leaving them detached from their reality in a void between two worlds. The least we can do as educators is make space for our students to be themselves as they communicate in authentic and comfortable ways.

Different Ways of Being and Knowing

In addition to communicating differently, anyone who has studied intercultural communication can attest to the fact that different cultures understand and interact with the world in different ways. Perhaps one of the greatest obstacles to effectively communicating with culturally diverse individuals is the tendency to apply one's own values to those with whom one interacts. As young children we learn the difference between right and wrong, what is deemed socially acceptable behavior, and methods of thought by all that surrounds us. Predominantly, we learn from our family, close friends, and community. As such, we learn from people who hold similar values and thought processes. Unfortunately, this means people tend to apply the same lessons they learned throughout life to those they encounter from other cultures. Frequently, the assumptions forming the foundation of thought for the individual do not apply to those with whom he or she is interacting.

There are a plethora of factors defining both individual and cultural identity. These differences affect how we see the world, understand the world, and communicate with others. Intercultural communication theorists point to such cultural outlooks and dispositions as: subjective versus objective, low context versus high context, low uncertainty versus high uncertainty, individualistic versus collectivistic, low power distance versus high power distance, masculine versus feminine, doing versus being, monochronic versus polychronic, and past versus present versus future. This is by no means an exhaustive list of the different orientations held by unique cultures. These perspectives shape the individual, how people interact with one another, and how they operate in the world.

Take for example the different perspectives on objectivity. Cultures take on either a predominately subjective or objective view of the world. In a subjective society, people tend to examine situations and make decisions based on their emotions or feelings.[7] These societies tend to be fatalistic, placing their lives in the hands of the *gods*. They may perceive the world as acting upon them rather than they upon it. Conversely, objective societies evaluate decisions and situations on the facts and apply systems of logic to problems rather than relying on instinctive reactions or emotional terms. As a result, individuals tend to believe they control their own destiny; and society tends toward the scientific and technological disciplines.[8]

Different cultures also break down along individualistic versus collectivistic orientations. Within highly individualistic societies like the dominant white culture in the United States, we preference the individual in almost all things. A person is expected to succeed on their own accord, individual merit is prized, and the rights of the individual are seen as paramount. Contrast that with collectivistic cultures, like those of Alaska Native peoples where the members of the community see their success as part of a communal effort and ask themselves what their obligations are toward the community rather than expecting the community to bend around the wants and desires of the individual.

Another dichotomy encompasses masculine versus feminine cultures. In masculine societies, individuals and organizations seek control of money, resources, power, and even other people. Virtually every major social, business, and political organization in the West is based on a strict, vertical organizational structure. As such, people are heard asking the questions *what's in it for me, how will I benefit,* or *how can I use this to my advantage*? Feminine cultures, however, take an alternative approach. Feminist Janice Jiggins explains that "women's vision includes nurturance rather than control, the management of networks of relationships rather than hierarchical dominance, and a concern for future generations as a guiding principle for today's decisions."[9] In short, this view centers itself on the principles of cooperation and mutual benefit, rather than the *power-centered* view prevalent in masculine societies.

Furthermore, cultures display different orientations focused either on the past, present, or future. Cultures centered on the past have a deep regard for history, tradition, and the elderly. Ultimately, they believe this "awareness of history" is essential "to an understanding of contemporary life."[10] Cultures emphasizing the present celebrate life and seek to make the most out of the present circumstances.[11] They live in the here and now. Lastly, some cultures focus on the future.[12] For example, the dominant white culture in the United States is heavily oriented toward the future, emphasizing such things as development, growth, and future profitability.

I do not have the space to fully explore the various cultural orientations and behaviors that we may confront. I merely hope to express that there are, in fact, differences that our students bring into the classroom. The lessons from intercultural communication for us are three-fold:

> People from different cultures experience the world (and even events) in unique ways that are shaped by the culture in which they live.
>
> People make sense of the world from unique perspectives and, thus, interpret events differently from those with different lived experiences.
>
> People share their experiences with others by communicating in different ways that are themselves shaped by their cultural viewpoints.

Unfortunately, this creates problems for us. The educational system in the United States was designed by and for the dominant white population. Willie Hensley, a prominent Alaska Native who helped create the Alaska Federation of Natives, once quoted missionary and political leader Sheldon Jackson who explained that the educational system was designed "to fit them for the social and industrial life of the white population of the United States and to promote their not-too-distant assimilation."[13] The system was designed to erase alternative cultural perspectives and indoctrinate all students into the dominant cultural orientations. Hensley explained that "the tragedy has been that the educational system which we have inherited . . . has also had as its basis the elimination of the Eskimo, the Indian, and the Aleut people as an identity, as a distinct species of the human race, with their own spirit, their own language, traditions, history, and culture."[14]

As educators, we must realize our classrooms are full of diverse students. They come to us with different orientations and values. In my teacher preparation program at the University of Alaska Anchorage, our first class was Paul Ongtooguk's Issues in Alaska Native Education. His class was designed to open the eyes of a predominantly white cohort of future teachers to the educational realities of our future Alaska Native students, which we could then extrapolate to students of other cultures. Thus, he flipped the classroom.

In a typical school setting, students from differing cultural backgrounds are plucked from their everyday lives and placed in an educational system designed by predominantly white policymakers, that conform to the desires of predominantly white school boards, and that are implemented by predominantly white teachers. While all those individuals may have genuinely good intentions, their frames of reference do not necessarily align with those of their students, families, and communities. We are guided by our white experience that is rooted in Euro-American cultural values and outlooks. Thus, our courses in teacher preparation programs obviously take that same approach.

So, Paul flipped the script. We were the ones taking a class that felt foreign. Paul intentionally operated on a different view of time. There was less focus on the individual. Discussions often connected to other topics in ways we did not anticipate. There was a high degree of uncertainty in the classroom, to name just a handful of departures from our previous experiences with Western education. The effect on our cohort ranged from uneasiness to anxiety to frustration and even anger (in one student's outburst at the degree of uncertainty). Given that we were all successful graduate students in our mid-twenties and beyond, one can only imagine how an elementary-age student, teenager, or undergraduate may feel and respond when their educational experience is quite a departure from the life they have lived up to that point.

The lessons were many, but as it is relevant to this text, I whittle it down to two central concepts:

Given the core differences in which we make sense of the world and share meaning with others based on our cultural identity, we must make an honest effort to allow students to explore ideas and communicate in culturally authentic ways.

Failure to make room for our student's cultural identities by mandating rigid conformity, forces them to slice off critical elements of who they are as human beings. Our goals should not be to replicate ourselves, but to foster their growth as *real human beings.*

We must recognize that not everyone experiences the world as we do. They see the world differently. They make sense of the world differently. They value different things. Success can be defined in vastly different ways by different cultures. Advancement for the individual at the expense of or even simply without concern for the community, for example, can feel hollow or even deemed an epic failure. As educators, we have a responsibility to understand where our students are coming from and make space for them to express themselves in culturally appropriate ways.

Building a Community of Learners

How then should we organize our schools? Writing in their book, *The Students Are Watching*, Theodore and Nancy Sizer explain that "to find the core of a school, don't look at its rulebook or even its mission statement. Look at the way the people in it spend their time—how they relate to each other, how they tangle with ideas . . . estimate the frequency and the honesty of its deliberations."[15] There is a lot to that quote, certainly, but one element that stands out to me is "how we relate to each other." What are the relationships like in the school: between the staff, between the students, and between staff and students?

The pursuit of knowledge in our schools is not defined by the content of our subjects either. In the *Courage to Teach*, Parker J. Palmer explains that the "hallmark of the community of truth is not psychological intimacy or political civility or pragmatic accountability . . . *reality is a web of communal relationships, and we can know reality only by being in community with it.*"[16] In short, to grow as individuals and to understand the world, we must form meaningful communities in our classrooms.

In a multicultural environment this begins by accepting and celebrating the differences we bring into the classroom. Fundamentally, we must resist the urge that arises when we feel challenged because of differences in communication. In a recent issue of *Teaching Tolerance*, educator and activist Charlie McGeehan was quoted as saying, "I have to actively resist the urge to maintain power or control in my classroom, and especially to resist the anger that can bubble up in me when that control is called into question . . . I actively work against these impulses in my practice—but even after years of doing this, it still takes work."[17] When we feel the emotional reaction of a perceived challenge to our authority, take a moment and breathe. Ask ourselves, what is really going on? Is there the possibility we are experiencing a miscommunication?

I remember my first day of visiting a classroom in the Saint Louis Urban Debate League when I took a position as the organization's program director. Two students at Soldan High School, Mohamud and Lekia, were loud, bouncing out of their seats, and constantly interrupting me. There were moments that I felt frustrated because I did not seem to have any control over the classroom. There were moments that I could feel the blood rushing to my face because I felt like I was failing in the moment. When my time in the classroom was over, I packed up my stuff and walked out the door. One of those two students—Mohamud—raced after me, shouting "*Mr. Shawn! Mr. Shawn!*" When I turned around, he said something to the effect of, "I'm really sorry if you thought my partner and I were rude. We're just so excited to debate this year! I hope you come back to class soon."

Thankfully, I did not feel personally attacked by their behaviors while I was teaching, nor did I respond with authoritarian mechanisms of control. Emotionally, I was challenged, but I kept thinking back to the lessons of George Henderson and Paul Ongtooguk. They had prepared me for situations like this, and I remembered that my perception was not the only reality present in that classroom. Recognizing those differences in communication is only part of the solution, however.

While working on my master's degree in teaching, I had the pleasure of taking three courses with Janet Steinhauser at the University of Alaska Anchorage. She made it a core tenet of her job to build a community of learners in the classroom. In that space, everyone's voice was welcome. She sought to create meaningful relationships between the students and with herself. In her classroom, this was a precondition for meaningful conversations about the content of the courses.

She spent countless hours in the classroom challenging us to work with one another so that we saw each other as collaborative members of a community. She took the time to get to know each of us on a personal level, making us feel valued. She reminded us that in the classroom, we serve our students and their communities. Some perspectives hold that students are vessels to be filled by the teacher, that the students answer to the teacher and the school. In reality, we are there to support them; therefore, we must make every effort to see and hear them as human beings.

The way she built her classroom left a profound impact on me. In my college classes, I now spend the first week of every semester working almost exclusively on building a community. Any content we cover is tangential to my efforts to build relationships with and between students. At first, this is met with skepticism and hesitation by most of my students, but ultimately it pays huge dividends as we progress throughout the semester. At a fundamental level, however, it is about respecting our students and truly valuing their contributions. We must make effort to let our students be heard and add their voice to our collective understanding of the world. Being an effective teacher requires compassion, empathy, and passion.

Conclusions

We have just as much responsibility to teach linguistic and cultural "minority" students as we do the dominant culture's students. All students should be afforded an equal opportunity to learn to the maximum extent possible. Furthermore, we can maximize the education of all our students by incorporating the views of those students who are different from one another. If our students are continually given a Eurocentric, white, middleclass American viewpoint, we—as a people—will fail to progress educationally; we will fail to truly understand the world. Simply, it is best for all to incorporate diversity at every possible opportunity, whether that means exposing the majority to the minority or vice versa.

As educators, we should strive to bring compassion into the classroom. Begin by recognizing that we all come into the classroom with different ways of communicating and respect those differences. As we develop lessons, value the different ways of being and knowing that exist in the communities we serve. Seek opportunities to allow students to express themselves and explore the content in culturally appropriate ways that cultivate authentic learning experiences. Finally, create spaces that welcome all students, foster meaningful interactions between students, and highlight the fact that we are all in this endeavor together.

What does that mean for us as debate coaches? Hopefully, the answer by now is obvious. Remember this is an educational activity. That premise should drive our actions more than competition. Make room for differences in the form of communication taken by students who enter the debate space. Welcome the perspectives of students and evidence that present alternative ways of knowing and being in the world. And, most importantly, strive to create a community by inviting authentic communication in the world of debate. The students stand before you, expressing themselves—daring to be themselves despite the risk that you will reject them. A risk that others may exclude them or devalue them for what is natural to them yet different from the "norm." Allow yourself to be moved. Allow yourself to truly listen to their authentic voices.

Notes

1. George Henderson, *Our Souls to Keep: Black/White Relations in America* (Yarmouth, ME: Intercultural Press, Inc., 1999), 112.

2. Henderson, 112.

3. Henderson, 116.

4. Henderson, 121.

5. Coshandra Dillard, "The Weaponization of Whiteness in Schools: It's Time to Recognize and Stop the Pattern," *Teaching Tolerance* 65, Fall 2020, np. https://www.tolerance.org/magazine/fall-2020/the-weaponization-of-whiteness-in-schools?fbclid=IwAR37fDLFRLICWc8QGHWKqHJGIYHJ8ivYusr0qviZy43W3E7i3OLYly9lPRk.

6. While it is thankfully becoming less frequent for students to be denied this right, there are indirect ways in which they are discouraged whether it be the teacher's nonverbal reaction or other defensive barriers erected by the instructor.

7. Thompson Dele Olasiji, "Intercultural Dimensions" (lectures presented for Human Relations 5110-108: International Human

Relations class, University of Oklahoma, Hurlburt Field, FL, July 12–14, 2004).

8. Olasiji.

9. Janice Jiggins, *Changing the Boundaries: Women-Centered Perspectives on Populations and the Environment* (Island Press, 1994), np.

10. Judith N. Martin and Thomas K. Nakayama, *Intercultural Communication in Contexts* (Boston, MA: McGraw-Hill, 2004), 93.

11. Martin and Nakayama.

12. Martin and Nakayama.

13. Willie Hensley, "Speech by Willie Hensley at Bilingual Conference" (speech, Anchorage, AK, February 1981), accessed November 29, 2020, www.alaskool.org/native-Ed/2hensley1.html.

14. Hensley.

15. Theodore R. Sizer and Nancy Faust Sizer, *The Students Are Watching: Schools and the Moral Contract* (Boston, MA: Beacon Press, 1999), 18.

16. Parker J. Palmer, *The Courage to Teach* (San Francisco, CA: Jossey-Bass, 1998), 95.

17. Dillard, np.

Section Four
Nontraditional Debate

The wolverine makes the northern lights burn at night.
He sets the northern lights on fire and
whenever he makes the northern lights burn, the
wolverine people are walking around.
That's the wolverine walking around at night.
 Yaadiimeey ("The Northern Lights"), as told by Mary
 Tyone of the Scottie Creek People

Historically, policy debate topics begin with a call to action by the United
States federal government. For over a hundred years, debaters have been
directed to place their trust in the government when defending the affirmative side of the topic.

In the 1990s and early 2000s, some debaters began to take issue with
that approach. They began to question whether the federal government
is or should be considered an appropriate actor at all. They examined
the legacy of various institutions enshrined in government or embraced
by it. They explored the blindness that existed within academic bodies
when those institutions published research or crafted the annual debate
topics. Who were the beneficiaries of the proposed courses of action?
Who was left out?

The debaters challenged the performative norms rewarded within the
debate community. Whose standards of dress were expected to be followed in competition? Whose accents, patterns of speech, and vocabulary

were expected? Whose ways of knowing and being in the world were used to determine the validity of one's thoughts?

More importantly, whose standards of dress, communication, and ways of knowing were punished for simply existing within the debate space?

In the early 2010s, the movement gained strength. It gained strength by recruiting more practitioners, and it gained strength by subverting the norms and conventions of the activity itself. Debaters began breaking the rules of communication norms within the activity, (*arguably*) the standards of evidence, and the directives of the annual debate topic and academic debate's governing bodies.

Rather than using the dominant white speech patterns, *some* embraced the dialects of their own communities. Rather than speaking at four hundred words per minute spouting highly technical forms of evidence, *some* embraced the communication of song, poetry, and dance. Rather than relying solely on "expert" testimony, *some* incorporated the authentic experiences of members of their own community—voices often ignored, glossed over, or actively silenced. Rather than argue in favor of action by the federal government, *some* blatantly argued against placing faith in those institutions.

In short, performance debate cannot be described as a singular performative style and is better viewed as a nontraditional approach to debate. It is a conglomeration of dispositions, styles, forms of communication, and even acts of defiance against the dominant power structures within the debate community and beyond. It is a revolutionary act, and its practitioners are fighting for recognition of their humanity and reform of a system that fails to fully live up to its ideals.

13.
The Constant Pursuit of Inclusivity

Nicole D. Nave

When asked to contribute to this book, the first topic I thought of was *performance debate*. As a former national debate champion who has been labeled by the term, this would be my opportunity to speak to the field of argumentation directly and unmask any mystery behind what performance debate truly is. To do that, I had to begin by identifying it.

I found myself troubled when attempting to define what performance debate is, simply because a static definition does not exist. Performance debate is a label used to respond to debaters that took a nontraditional approach to a resolution-based discussion by refusing to advocate for the United States federal government's actions. Performance debate exists as a term to label and stigmatize debaters who cause chaos by straying away from the dominant rhetorical standards of what speaking styles debaters "should" utilize. As a former director, coach, and debater who identifies as Black, woman, poor, and queer, I found my experience within this activity unique because I refused to reproduce traditional rhetorical styles of policy engagement.

I will argue that *performance debate*, as a category meant to define debaters who refuse traditional debate engagement, is a polarizing term meant to invalidate the academic contributions of those debaters labeled as such.

Validation of similar terms has been utilized as divisive rhetoric to demar-
cate Black participant's academic contributions to the activity. Through this
chapter, I hope to defy the underlying racist, sexist, ableist, and classist logic
that riddles the field of argumentation and debate when referring to these
rhetorical artifacts that have been labeled by the term.

Performance Debate as Praxis

Performance debate was produced as a term of art in response to the stylistic shift in Black argumentation known as the Louisville Project. An examination of the practices of the project is crucial to understanding how
the label "performance debate" came to exist. The challenge of rhetorical
styles in all forms that are present in performance debate is a worthwhile
praxis implied in the foundation of the speaking principles: ethos, pathos,
and logos. Thus, performance debaters upheld the soundest foundations of
rhetoric and produced a pedagogical model for democratic deliberation and
education comparable to traditional debate engagement.

An analysis of the benefits of defying the dominant forum of debate
provides a significant perspective for the study of increasingly diverse styles
of argumentation. This research requires the admission of stylistic divides
influenced by but not limited to racism, sexism, ableism, and classism. To
thoroughly examine why the term performance debate poses such a challenge to competitive debate, research must account for the intersections that
maintain and contribute to the gaps within the debate activity.

Performance debate has been emerging across multiple forums of the
activity for over a decade. After collegiate policy debate's introduction to
performance debate, the term began to appear on debate forums such as
Debate Central, Cross-EX.com, CEDAforum, and other small subset debate
communities after Emporia State "united the crowns" in 2013. When debaters choose not to follow the normative policy-making style of engagement,
they are labeled and defined by their methods as *performance debaters.*
The current director of the Malcolm X Debate Society at the University of
Louisville, Dr. Tiffany Dillard-Knox, points out that alternative forms of
debate are known for engaging in unique styles. "The presentation of argument in alternative debates can encompass the performance of rap music,
poetry, metaphors and other art forms during a round (Polson, 2012)."[1] After
pioneering alternative styles of debate, the University of Louisville remains
a locus to performance-style debate. A historical analysis of the University

of Louisville's engagement in policy debate is necessary to fully encapsulate the rhetorical potential of performance debate.

The Louisville Project

In 2008, the University of Louisville's debate team took collegiate debate by storm, creating the historical foundation for debaters who resist stylistic norms through performance debate. In the article "Voice Dipped in Black: The Louisville Project and the Birth of Black Radical Argument in College Policy Debate," Dr. Shanara Reid-Brinkley describes the details behind the "Louisville Project." She says:

> The University of Louisville's Malcolm X Debate Program, a mostly Black student group, founded a small grassroots movement in competitive college debate . . . Louisville battled a resistant majority-white academic community for years . . . During their winning 2003–2004 season, the team transformed into what became commonly referred to as the Louisville Project. The development of an acclaimed Louisville Method of Debate would have significant reverberations through both the college and high school debate communities more than fifteen years later. Troubling the assumption of neutrality, Louisville's performance and argumentation highlight the hypocrisy of traditional debate performance, its relationship to anti-Blackness, and the normative performance of whiteness as the marker of achievement. The Louisville team delves into the neoliberal ordering of American democracy, making visible the hypocrisy of white liberalism and its attendant antagonism—subtle and overt—toward Blackness . . . consider how the embodiment of Blackness critically affects the reading of voice . . . Does the Black, particularly the Black that performs Blackness, have voice in a civil society constituted by anti-Blackness.[2]

Performances similar to those of the participants of the Louisville Project have continued to increase in debate as dynamic styles of nontraditional engagement continue to present themselves. However, as performance debate grows in popularity, students that employ these styles of engagement are targeted by harsh racial criticism and are negatively labeled with derogatory markers. Dr. Dillard-Knox explained the creation of these markers and its negative implications. "While the 'Louisville Project' is how most people refer to the new methods that Louisville debate program would eventually develop, the word 'project' implies something that is temporal and/or experimental. However, thirteen years later, it is neither of those things."[3]

Distinct actions that became essential to this new category of debate included critiquing the whiteness of argumentation and rhetoric as well as challenging stylistic traditions of college policy debate like spreading and resolution-focused debate.[4] Dillard-Knox explains, "The argument was that speed reading made the activity inaccessible to those not trained in debate, including new debaters and anyone that may be interested in viewing a debate, such as parents or the staff on the campuses where debates took place. Additionally, the team would find a racial perspective from which to debate the topic. In other words, whatever the topic, the team would find an argument related to the perspective of Blacks."[5] By refusing norms, Black debaters explored alternative formats of debate distinct from traditional forms of argumentation thus shifting the terms of role playing. Simply, "reliance on so-called expert evidence also contributed to disparity between those teams who had the coaching resources to complete extensive research and those who did not . . . The three-tier methodology" introduced by Louisville debaters opened academic debate to a "process of argumentation tapping into diverse forms of knowledge-making practices."[6]

> The three-tier process includes personal experience, organic intel-lectuals, and academic intellectuals. According to Nathan Abrams (1995), *organic intellectuals* have four characteristics. They must be a member of an "aggrieved community." As members of an aggrieved community, they should reflect the needs of that community. Thirdly, they attempt to challenge the power structures through the dissemi-nation of subversive ideas. The final characteristic is that they strive to construct an "historical block"—a coalition of oppositional groups united around these subversive ideas. *Academic intellectuals* are aca-demic experts in a particular field of research whose work is published in scholarly journals, non-fiction books, and other scholarly work, such as: theses, dissertations, and conference papers. Bartanen (1995) has described this type of knowledge as "authoritative evidence from an objective source."[7]

Engaging in a three-tier process advanced the participation of Black debaters by creating new opportunities for competitive success. Deven Cooper and

Dayvon Love, both from Baltimore City, transformed the college debate community as Towson University students when in 2008 they won the Cross Examination Debate Association (CEDA) National Debate Championship. This was the first time a team of Black college debaters had accomplished such a feat in the history of policy debate. Victories incorporating "project debate" like Towson's Championship prepared future generations of Black debaters for an era of growing and sustainable success. Louisville's utilization of the three-tier process provided the blueprint for future debaters to construct their own style of engagement in debate, creating a new era for Black debaters who strayed from the traditional centering of competition invoked by traditional policy debate. Many Black debaters developed alternative methods of incorporating the three-tier process into their arguments, which transcended the traditions of collegiate policy debate, thus rendering a noticeable shift to Black debaters' participation in the activity.

Uniting the Crowns

Inspired by the Louisville Project, "There have been several schools, such as Towson University, Oklahoma University, and the University of California State-Long Beach, as well as individual debaters that have adopted the three tier methodology (with and without the use of the metaphor) and applied it to various goals over the years."[8] Though many engaged in the process, the National Debate Tournament (NDT) champions remained white until Emporia State University's historic performance in 2013 provided an eccentric example for the future of performance debate. The Emporia State team of Ryan Wash and Elijah Smith united the crowns for the first time by winning both the NDT and the CEDA National Championships. "Their victory is one of many firsts: Last week Elijah & Ryan won the 2013 Cross Examination Debate Association national tournament (CEDA), making it the first time the same partnership won both college national championships in the same season."[9] The affirmative utilized the movie *The Wiz* as its central art of focus in which Wash compared his experience as a Black queer man in the debate activity to the experience of Diana Ross in the film. Wash described his experiences as an openly gay Black debater and how his social location influenced his overall relationship with the activity. Using the metaphorical approach to the resolution, Wash explained energy as a metaphor to how people who are marginalized by the activity of debate are unable to find themselves energized enough to feel like members of the community. By citing examples of exclusion in competitive success and the invalidation of argumentation Black debaters had experienced, Wash described how even the resolution had been used to prioritize a conversation about energy rather than the effects literal energy has on people's ability to participate not just in debate but in life. Wash explains watching members of his family sometimes "unable to produce enough energy to get out of bed in the morning." Infusing narrative and stories from the film, Wash's affirmative took a metaphorical approach to the resolution:

> Resolved: The United States Federal Government should substantially reduce restrictions on and/or substantially increase financial incentives for energy production in the United States of one or more of the following: coal, crude oil, natural gas, nuclear power, solar power, wind power.

This strategy of combining theory and experience tailored aspects of the three-tier process to accompany the methodological practices of "Quare theory" by theorist E. Patrick Johnson. Wash utilized the rhetorical tool of *home* to convey the tensions Black debaters experienced in the activity. Johnson's theory explains that "homeplace is a site which quare praxis must critique. That is, we may seek refuge in homeplace as a marginally safe place to critique oppression outside its confines, but we must also deploy Quare theory to address oppression within homeplace itself."[10] For Wash and Smith, deploying Quare theory in debate incorporated the academic intellectualism the three-tier process required for participants to connect academic discourse to personal experience.

Like the debaters of Louisville, Emporia State's Wash and Smith received negative backlash for their performance, which sought to highlight the division of the debate community based on debaters' stylistic preferences. Dividing debaters and labeling them by the style of argumentation they participate in has continued to be a divisive strategy to otherize nontraditional forms of argument.

Backlash

Many in both the collegiate and high school debate community have become familiar with the term performance debate. Defining what performance debate truly is would require us to ignore the racially charged history around the creation of the phrase. A thorough historical analysis would identify the mischaracterization of the rhetorical strategy as merely a performance rather than a productive exchange of political advocacy. This label discredits those who have, are, and plan to engage in nontraditional debate performances.

In an article titled "Performance Debates: How to Defend Yourself," the author defines performance debate as "an affirmative that does not have a plan and claims that the value of their speech act comes before traditional policymaking concerns."[11] This article is one of many from high school coaches in response to an influx of debaters refusing to participate in traditional forms of political role playing in favor of performance debate. Heidt says, "I enjoyed reading about critical theory in graduate school and believe people when they claim that this literature has opened up new ways of looking at the world. At the same time, I cannot imagine telling a classroom full of new ninth-grade debaters that instead of debating public policy that they need to learn about a very specialized and alien-sounding slice of academic literature."[12]

Reductionist attitudes toward the breaks from traditional models of policy debate have manifested tension toward students labeled performance debaters. In an article titled "The Racial Coding of *Performance Debate*: Race, Difference, and Policy Debate," the author Nick Scullio addressed the similar dismissal of argumentative validation in the debate activity. Scullio says,

> *Performance debate* is the racially-coded language that devalues black participation in debate, and that, along with the label's lack of benefit for coaching or thinking about debate arguments or strategy, warrants its dismissal from everyday use. Not only is it racially coded and unhelpful, but it also disincentivizes black participation which is always rendered as other. Racially coded rhetoric is a particularly insidious way to express racist ideas under the guise of race-neutral language. As such, one way to express displeasure with or a distaste for black debaters, and to discourage their participation, is to describe *their* debate as *performance debate* as opposed to *debate*.[13]

Scullio's analysis provides critical insight into the division within the debate community writ large. The analysis exposes the uncomfortable reality that debate has been racially motivated to categorize rhetorical styles as a method of devaluing the ones that minority debaters have a proclivity toward. Online forums dedicated to debate provide a space for anonymous rhetorical violence targeted at performance debaters. Comment sections are riddled with accounts calling performance debaters cheaters and bullies. Such coding implies that to perform in debate opens you up to real-world violence that is avoidable when role playing as a policymaker. Such comments ironically ignore the similar acts of violence that occur daily with respect to the very minority students who participate in the activity and have their identity challenged, dismissed, erased, and/or punished for simply existing within the debate space.

Debate Is Debate

Divide and conquer has been a strategy of dominating marginalized people for generations. Debate, as a microcosm of the world, participates in the division by individualizing styles of argumentation to represent debaters' identities. Performance debate as a term represents the shift from the identification that Louisville was not a project but a continuation of alternative forms of argumentation. Black debaters provide a unique avenue for representation through academic discourse by circulating critical race scholarship throughout the academy and their communities by reading these authors during debate rounds. Black debaters' use of this scholarship also validates the work of Black academics who systematically are not given the same respect as their White contemporaries. Black debaters not only circulate Black scholars, but they also create original Black artifacts distinct from what the academy has deemed as evidence. Black debaters rupture biased standards of communication by disrupting what can qualify as evidence and exposing the systems that contribute to the impossibility of Black people ever fully being included in a community rooted in whiteness.

Not only has debate seen an increase in the diversity of scholarship, but it has also seen an increase in the participation and competitive success of Black debaters as several CEDA championships have now had with Black winners. This is particularly true for Black women.

2014—Towson University—Ameena Ruffin and Korey Johnson
2015—Towson University—Troi Thomas and Kevin Whitley
2016—University of Vermont—Khalil Lee
2017—Rutgers University-Newark—Devane Murphy and Nicole
    D. Nave

2018—University of Iowa—Geo Liriano, Coco Christopherson,
  and Brooke Kimbrough
2019—University of Oklahoma—Darius White and Jazmine
  Pickens[14]

The NDT remains an elitist forum where Black debaters have not seen the same amount of competitive success. There have only been two Black women to ever win the title: myself, in 2017, and Quaram Robinson in 2018.[15] Quaram Robinson also became the first Black woman to win the Rex Copeland Award. The Rex Copeland Memorial Award is presented annually to the collegiate debate team ranked number one in the first round, at-large team selections. Not only have Black debaters seen limited success at the NDT compared to CEDA, but the success of Black debaters at CEDA has been weaponized to devalue the credentials of the tournament. Decrease in participants over the years has shown major decline in the legitimacy of CEDA as a national championship post Black debaters becoming consistently successful. Not only do students see limited success in deep elimination rounds of the NDT, but Black coaches and judges make up a small fraction of the judging pool. Inevitably, this leads to divides that segregate thought and argumentation within the community. Stopping such backlash requires us to view debaters as debaters, not as the arguments they participate in. Performance debate only exists as a rebranded term post-Louisville project to orchestrate inclusion. However, these divisions only further create subsets within the debate community. On one side are those that rely on dogmatism to advance the concept that policy debate is only valuable when it is centered around the United States federal government and its policies. On the other side are those that defend Black debaters' ability to choose how to approach the topic. Ending rhetorical divisiveness in judging paradigms, arguments, and research can cause a necessary shift for actual inclusion in debate.

Conclusion

While the term performance debate has negative historical connotations, participants who dare to defy the rhetorical style of traditional policy debate provide a unique benefit to the debate community. The deployment of social location as a framework for political engagement produces a break from the normative narrative of what constitutes a policy debate. The founding fathers of rhetoric envisioned performance debate when discussing the necessity of deliberative democracy. The educational benefits of students who defied debate norms are the highlight of Dr. Reid-Brinkley's thesis, "Ghetto Kid Gone Good."[16] For debaters like me that have chosen to engage outside the lines rhetorically, performance debate produces an intrinsic value outside of structures of policy debate to validate the contribution that experience can provide for exploring and understanding a myriad of issues. Only understanding debate beyond the competitive aspects will allow an understanding of the importance of alternative styles of engagement in argumentation. Overall, Black debaters' contributions disrupt the academy's narrative of what is evidential and what is not—carving out opportunities for future generations of Black debaters to redefine advocacy for themselves on their own terms. Rewriting the rules for policy debate has always been a controversial task only achievable with the Black subjects who are willing to contribute the work.

Notes

1. Tiffany Yvonne Dillard-Knox, "Against the Grain: The Challenges of Black Discourse within Intercollegiate Policy Debate." (master's thesis, University of Louisville, 2014) *Electronic Theses and Dissertations*, Paper 2161, 2014, 20. https://doi.org/10.18297/etd/2161.

2. Shanara R. Reid-Brinkley, "Voice Dipped in Black: The Louisville Project and the Birth of Black Radical Argument in College Policy Debate." In *The Oxford Handbook of Voice Studies*, edited by Nina Sun Eidsheim and Katherine Meizel (Oxford: Oxford University Press, 2019), 215–16.

3. Dillard-Knox, 37.

4. Students who abandon the practice of resolution-focused debate address alternative issues they deem far more important to the participants and/or society.

5. Dillard-Knox, 37–38.

6. Reid-Brinkley, 223.

7. Dillard-Knox, 19.

8. Dillard-Knox, 47.

9. National Symposium for Debate. "Emporia State University Makes Collegiate Policy Debate History." *NSD Update*, April 2, 2013. http://nsdupdate.com/2013/emporia-state-university-makes-collegiate-policy-debate-history-wins-ndt-and-ceda/.

10. E. Patrick Johnson, "'Quare' Studies, or (Almost) Everything I Know about Queer Studies I Learned from My Grandmother." *Text and Performance Quarterly* 21, no. 1 (2001): 1–25. http://dx.doi.org/10.1080/10462930128119.

11. Jenny Heidt, "Performance Debates: How to Defend Yourself." *Rostrum*, April 2003, accessed May 25, 2020, https://debate.uvm.edu/NFL/rostrumlib /cxHeidtcx0403.pdf.

12. Heidt.

13. Nick J. Sciullo, "The Racial Coding of Performance Debate: Race, Difference, and Policy Debate." *Argumentation and Advocacy* 55, no. 4 (October 12, 2019): 303–21. DOI: 10.1080/10511431.2019.1672028.

14. *Editor's note*: The author wrote this chapter during the pandemic, around the time of the 2021 national championships. Since that time, the CEDA national championship has been won by Zach Watts and Het Desai (University of Texas, 2021), Asya Taylor and Dimarvin Puerto (Wake Forest University, 2022), and Iyana Trotman and Tajaih Robinson (Wake Forest University, 2023).

15. *Editor's note*: Iyana Trotman and Tajaih Robinson, like the author Nicole D. Nave, successfully united the crowns in 2023.

16. Shanara Rose Reid-Brinkley, "Ghetto Kids Gone Good: Race, Representation, and Authority in the Scripting of Inner-City Youths in the Urban Debate League." *Argumentation and Advocacy* 49, no. 2 (February 2, 2017): 77–99. https://doi.org/10.1080/00028533.2012.11821781.

14.
Living Inupiat Storytelling in Four Generations of Family

Paul Ongtooguk and Pulgeenok
Methanie Ongtooguk

This is the only chapter in this volume by authors without competitive debate experience. In fact, Paul Ongtooguk has been skeptical of this competitive activity since we met. Then, why this chapter, and why these contributors? I met Paul in graduate school at the University of Alaska Anchorage. One of our first classes was Paul's Issues in Alaska Native Education. I immediately found him to be one of the most unique and best instructors I had ever had to include my undergraduate at the United States Air Force Academy and a previous graduate degree from the University of Oklahoma. The lessons he conveyed were numerous. One thing I fell in love with, though, was his ability to teach through stories. In nontraditional approaches to debate, students frequently use stories to communicate. These stories may be known worldwide as told by famous artists, singers, writers, or activists. Alternatively, they may be deeply personal stories, written by the students themselves. There are big stories about history, sociology, economics, and international relations. There are little stories about relationships, community, and people. Regardless, they are important stories with important lessons. I asked Paul to contribute to this work as a professor of education who

understands our role as teachers. I asked Paul to contribute to this work
as someone from a culture that shares wisdom through stories. I asked
Paul to contribute to this work because he understands the nature of
story and its role in education and the world.—Shawn Briscoe

For the Inupiat of Alaska, or northern Inuit, the traditional culture lives through storytelling. In the story, we find perspective and markers of conduct. We learn how to use humor as a way to deal with hardship, mistakes, and anger. We learn to respect our Elders who serve as guides to essential knowledge about tribal existence. Story develops relational knowledge—our place in the world, the community within ourselves. Story is cultural memory, entertainment, and a context for community decision-making. Most importantly, storytelling releases the power of imagination which is one of the most powerful tools Raven shared with humans.

In this brief essay we can only peek into this great room of story and look at a few pieces. We are going to mix things up by starting with a description of Inupiat storytelling by using some of our ways of storytelling. This may or may not work. That is for you to imagine and decide.

Storytelling has been a part of how the Inupiat people have lived since before Western history began. For perspective, we were living in the Arctic before Alexander the Great looked on the Euphrates River. When contextualizing themselves, European scholars determined that the written word epitomized the beginning of civilization. Writing was the first sign of carried intelligence over generations versus the daily fight for survival from the Western view. In their zeal to "map" the world, European scholars made the written word the demarcation line of whether a previously uncontacted people were, in fact, *people*. These cultures, without the written word, would become *prehistory* or *prehistorical peoples* in the annals of Western historical scholarship. This effectively segregated cultures: those within and outside of European "civilization."

European history often tells a narrative about how we, Inupiat, wandered about stumbling upon plants, useful stones, and animals to kill. But wandering across lands and waters is like buying lottery tickets as an income strategy. While some riches may appear, the odds do not favor sustaining and growing a culture over generations. Instead of magical wandering, traditional life is living in a cycle in line with seasonal abundance. Foods and resources tend to show up quickly and in abundance but only briefly. The key is to know when and where that abundance of blueberries, red salmon, whitefish, walrus, whale, parka squirrels, fattened marmot, silver salmon, and many, many other gifts of the world can be found to provide for those who are ready and who show appreciation. This was not simply happenstance. In the following story excerpt, we can see how observation, careful consideration, and respect for the natural world and its inhabitants are equivalent.

The village was always listening; looking closely at the animals, plants, and checking the waters for fish, seal, and whale. Looking at snow conditions; how firm the ground was for travel and then how firm the ground was for travel after the spring melt and following storms.

In this life, Mocoluq was out with her friends collecting rocks that would be perfect in hardness, without being brittle, to make into digging tools for tasty kinds of roots. They heard bawling and crying noises. They carefully went to check and saw there was a little bear cub that had fallen into a deep cut on the cliff side.

The mother bear was watching the cub. The cliff was too steep for her and she had a sibling cub with her. Considering the predicament, Mocoluq calmly told the mother bear she was going to slowly and gently pull the cub out of the spot. It was difficult to climb into the narrow cut. She barely squeezed in and finally wrapped the cub in a caribou skin so it would not scratch her with its sharp little claws. It stopped bawling and being tired, curled up in the blanket.

Mocoluq then walked over to a spot where she could climb up the cliff. It was very steep, sharp, and slippery. When she approached the top of the cliff, she lifted the cub up onto the grassy ledge. The cub rushed out of the caribou hide and called for the mother bear.

As Mocoluq slipped and slid down the cliff and reached the bottom, she looked up and saw the mother bear with both of her cubs safely with her. The mother bear acknowledged Mocoluq by dipping her head.

For years following, in the spring when the snow was melting and the birds were calling overhead, Mocoluq would often find roots dug up in her favorite spot, waiting for her. The claw and paw prints of a large bear all around, outlined by smaller ones.

Whenever they saw each other, Mocoluq and the mother bear would stop and slowly nod their heads at each other. In the fall, Mocoluq would see the mother bear and leave a nice pile of berries that she shared from both her picking and the village. The mother bear would wait, and then enjoy the berries Mocoluq shared.

Storytelling prepares us for our travels in a wide range of regions, psychological and physical: wind-blown islands, expanses of tundra, woodlands of birch and pine, ice bound coasts. Storytelling also prepares for moral dangers: impatience and urgency, greed, selfishness, individualism, lacking respect, wrongful exclusion, and disproportionate pride. Inupiat lands, waters, and homelands. Storytelling tends to reach a high point during the long nights of winter. Stories are mixed into story dances, Elders telling long-form stories might go two weeks or more. Other stories are for children and can be told in a couple of minutes. Stories can be told for prime-age persons, both men and women, about their skills and to shape their heart for dealing with inevitable hardships and mistakes. Many stories warn of a very dangerous event—success—and prepare us for the failure that often befalls achievement.

However, even our *shared* experiences with the West in the institutions—schools and language—that convey our history to others, fail to truly tell the stories in ways that capture the truth. When I (Paul) was a visiting teacher at the University of Pennsylvania, I recall graduate students and myself being confused about residential boarding schools for American Indians and Alaska Natives. They were connecting it to private boarding schools they knew about on the East Coast. With the Sherman Institute Indian Boarding School in Riverside, California, they had student last names who were clearly Inuit from Alaska Native villages in their student graveyard. The graduate students were silent when I talked about that as the private boarding schools on the East Coast normally did not have student cemeteries.

We also had confusion about the difference of traditional Alaska Native fish camps and summer camps on the East Coast. They assumed fish camp was like a week or two spent away from home with friends rather than picturing a summer of work with family while connecting with one another and the land. I learned a lot from those graduate students the first summer about where confusion points might exist given our different histories.

These confusion points exist about history in general. It is more than facts; it is personal and cultural windows by which we look at history as well. We must have honest conversations with one another if we are to have a meaningful understanding of our shared history—its legacy and its continued imprint upon our lives and our understanding.

Our culture is immersed and bound by story. Through story a trajectory of our people is transmitted. Time is not viewed chronologically, as in Western history, but as more of a spiral that winds and twists its way through space from the past to the present. Stories open threads within this spiral and we travel through seasons and the cycle of time so that we know when and where to find and appreciate the abundance that nature provides. Some of our most important stories are about disasters our ancestors have faced and how they survived.

We have flood accounts that overlap in some ways with the Bible version but also differ in important ways. For us, humans are not the center of the world. We know that the Arctic did fine before humans and that it will do fine without humans.

Fundamentally, our stories focus on the attitudes that lead to survival and success. We accept that humans are physically inferior and awkward, especially in comparison to many animals. We believe that our key gift is our minds and with that, our power of imagination. Our stories tell about the importance of our thoughts and our thinking through things, but often they also require us to use imagination and thought to sort out the stories themselves. In this way, they reflect our view of time as a spiral projection rather than a straight line. Western minds often dismiss our stories as deficient in plot and lacking key points of drama and conclusion. It is true that our stories do lack explicit summation. The storyteller does not explain the story in a tidy ending. How would that develop the mind of the listener? Those hearing the story must pull the pieces together and ponder the meaning and the lessons.

In our versions of the flood, human behavior has no connection to the cause of the flood. There is no supreme being who uses the flood to teach us a moral lesson. The understanding conveyed by the story is that there will be a flood. Some people will read signs of a coming flood; some will have ancestors who used natural signs as a warning of a flood. Sometimes there is a mysterious person teaching us about the flood, how to think and plan accordingly for such a disaster. It is about the growth of our minds that occurs after each major disaster. In our accounts, many include the descriptions of the bodies of a drowned animal swelling up and then floating on top of the waters. I can always smell that part of the story, and I like how our stories reward the more careful and detailed observations. Detailed observation is essential to life in the Arctic, and essential to story in ways that seem like needless flutter when trying to convey them in writing.

In our storytelling, there is time and again, a reward in finding humor in the most difficult hardships and disappointments. This often seems odd to outsiders, but cultural survival greatly increases when you can distance your mind enough from the situation to see the folly of yourself and others that brought you to this. If the mind can move away from the grip of hardship, then it is free to look around, think about what has happened, and imagine the right tools for solving the problem. There are many stories about conflict between and among people and how it must be vented and sorted out so that it does not become larger and poisonous. And here is an example of using story to solve a problem. If two people are having persistently hard feelings, they are invited to make a story song about the other person. In their story, they will tease the shortcomings of the other. Each performs their story song for the community and the one that gets the most laughter is the winner. The loser is expected to give the winner a gift that balances things and the community expectation is that the grievance and hard feelings are to be left there. If either brings it back up they may be ignored as though they do not really exist.

Stories are open ended and complex. It is possible and the best stories often can be understood to make multiple points and perhaps, depending on your own thoughts, you will draw different lessons from them. Our stories might be told in a structure like our traditional dances with a light review of the story and then a detailed review of the story, often followed by an individual way of shaping the story. If the individual, or artistic version, of the story is very popular then the name of that person and their version would enter the community treasure.

Our stories do not avoid hardships or tragedy or the details that accompany such events. They can be much more frightening than stories typically told to American children today. They are also clearly based in a culture that prides itself in the study of the physical, spiritual, and mindful aspects of humans. The best of our stories, often without fanfare or distinction, simply see the little things in the way of the interconnected spirals of the natural, spiritual world and accept these as a whole. The great room of Inupiat story awaits those who enter with minds that are open to learn, to be entertained, to reflect, and to develop the great power of the imagination as gifted to us by Raven.

15.
Defining Black Cards

Jamal Burns

There is one simple truth to policy debate: it is a two versus two style of competitive argumentation. Meaning then, it requires a partner, and, preferably, partners with equal levels of engagement and commitment to the activity. This fact posed much more difficulty for me than one would originally expect. Entering my senior year—my third year of debate—I had had three competitive partners in the event, all of whom had quit. Two weeks prior to the start of my final high school season, my fourth partner would soon reach the same conclusion as the partners before her: debate was not an activity that reflected her identity.

Hearing her repudiation of the activity disheartened me. Initially, my competitive spirit went into overdrive: how was I going to make it to nationals without a partner? However, when I inquired as to why she dismissed the activity, her response illuminated many of the inconsistencies with the spirit of debate that I held.

> Every tournament we've had, we have the same complaints. We have the same criticisms. We know that they are just going to continuously

give the wins to the white kids. To the kids from *that* high school. What's the use?

What was the use? Had I senselessly given myself to an activity that I criticized time and time again for not giving itself to me? Truly, I had the same qualms as she, yet I continued. Had I been oblivious to my own misgivings? I wrestled with these conversations. Not only was I tired of the gross mistreatment I received as a competitor, but I was tired of conforming every fiber of my being to fit the mold of what a good debater *should* be.

After much examination and thorough conversations with my prior partners, coaches, and friends, I decided to continue with the activity, but not without a *few* modifications. I was set to do a performance style of debate. This way, I could bring my identity into the matrix. To do this, I knew I had to partially—if not entirely—disengage with the system of debate that I knew.

Thus emerged my performance, "Defining Black Cards," where instead of using cards—the most quintessential form of evidence in debate—I discussed only stories of my life and how it influenced the interactions that occurred within debate. In my mind, it was essential to get rid of cards entirely. Cards represented a form of gate-kept knowledge, where those with the highest access to resources were able to acquire more robust collections of evidence to use in future debate rounds.

Cards also, unknowingly, presented evidence that was strikingly white. These pieces of evidence were white on three dimensions—*literal white*, meaning they were written by white authors; *commodified white*, meaning cards written by nonwhite authors were used to bolster the "diversity" portfolio of a case and their inclusion was in part related to the tokenization of the author and their ideals; and *proximally white*, meaning the evidence was written by highly educated nonwhite scholars who were educated at predominately white institutions. Now, this last category may appear strange.

However, we do know that institutions of higher learning have historically denied nonwhite students and have worked to maintain Eurocentric pedagogical models even after the admission of these students began. On an evidentiary level, it must be true that their value in debate is linked, at least partially, to their approximation to whiteness and white spaces. This by no means devalues the inherent blackness/otherness of each scholar's work, but it does suggest that in a predominately white space, there exists a cognitive reliance on white dominance to be considered credible. These categories are neither mutually exclusive nor dependent, but they typically work in tandem with one another to ensure impermeability to the then-current model of debate I participated in during high school.

This transition created a space where I, as a marginalized person, could openly express myself. At the core of this performance was a journey of self-discovery. I attempted to define, not redefine, my existence. For a re-definition would assume that a basis existed. It implies that I simply reused the same semantic code that was given to me by the systems that work to oppress me, and I was instead attempting to forge anew. This style of debate was obscure for my league. Many of the students who participated in debate followed its strict, didactic structure with little question on how it influenced them. As expected, the response to this performance was varied. I received comments that were disparagingly critical and others of high praise, but the latter were few and far between. The criticisms came from all sides: competitors, judges, and coaches. Individuals who were white, Asian, Black. Eventually, despite the variance in attitude toward the piece, I managed to acquire another partner—Taylor—who empathized with its message.

Taylor was one of my closest friends in high school, if not my closest. A Black woman who aspired to be a medical professional, Taylor was no stranger to the stifling of her voice. Her addition affixed a layer of complex-ity and utility that I could not, and this was a necessary feature. It allowed those hearing the debate to understand the plight of a low-income, Black woman that I could not convey as a low-income, queer, mixed-Black person. As the season progressed, we accumulated many more losses than wins. In fact, once we implemented this approach, we went 1–3 at every tournament except one in our region. But this was no longer about scoreboards, instead it was about the amplification of voice. Though, it would be disingenuous to say that each loss had no effect on me. In capitalist systems, you are an extension of what you produce. When one decides to present stories of their lives that are later discounted, it most surely will be discouraging, especially at the age of seventeen.

Criticisms of our performance followed two general formulas: "I un-derstand what you're saying, but I can't feel you" and "This is not the place for that." In other words, there was a cognitive dissonance between our lived experience and that of our predominantly white judges. One that told them that our avenue of performance was a mere abstract experiment for gain, instead of a legitimate critique of debate. It is this constant devaluing of performance debate as uninterpretable, misplaced, or inauthentic that detracts from the meaningfulness of the activity for particular students.

The students who are not allowed to fully enjoy the activity have yet to see or hear themselves in the debate narrative. Coming from disparate circumstances and living below the poverty line, my experiences as a debater centered difference. Where other debaters were reading from laptops, I had no internet activity. Where other debaters had debate camps, I had summer jobs. So, it was not unusual to see more resourced debaters deploy the trade secrets of debate camp or utilize a case cluttered with inaccessible language that they studied under the tutelage of the brightest minds at Kansas or Michigan debate camps, not for the transposition of knowledge, but for gain.

The common argument we faced was that there existed alternative sources to researching information. I would be remiss not to discuss the fallacies that exist in such a claim. The first is that, whether or not alternative methods to studying exist, these alternative methods are considerably defunct compared to their counterparts. Further, the quickest rebuttal was to use a free, public library to access information. This would be ideal if most library computers did not require a patron to have a library card to access them. Why is library card access an issue? Most states require a permanent address to sign up for one. With an issue as fervent as child homelessness, this response is woefully ignorant of the realities that many students face. Housing insecurity—which I was no stranger to—is but a form of disenfranchisement millions of students encounter. This haphazard response is an attempt to obfuscate one's own privilege. If one feels that there exist alternative avenues to achieve the same outcome, they will create a levelized field in their mind, no matter how distinctly different these methods may be. After all, we all existed within the same debate space, and that must have significant meaning.

Debate space is a common phrase one will hear between and within rounds. It is used to describe the interactivity between debaters, coaches, and judges that is palpable during tournaments. More than a phrase, however, the debate space is a physical state with amorphous properties. That is, each student will experience the activity of debate differently. However, the commonalities between the stories of splendor and stories of strife paint a grim tale of who is allowed to enjoy the activity. Now, the laborious and near impossible task of transforming this uniquely physical experience into one that could allow all to empathize fell on the laps of me and Taylor. We theorized numerous possibilities and meticulously considered their authenticity to our message. Ultimately, in one of our final tournaments of the season, we developed the Defining Black Cards piece and ensured that we did more than share our thoughts regarding our experiences—we enacted those experiences.

We became the debate space. I represented the desire to break free from the mold of an oppressive system, by expressing my frustration, anguish, and anger at the many ways the debate space disenfranchised me and those who looked like me. Taylor represented the current ways the system acts against marginalized bodies, by explaining the depths to which the system sidelines individuals of color throughout society. True to the word performance, we added movements and fluidity to our words. One of the most memorable aspects of this performance was a scene where I removed my buttoned-up shirt and tie to reveal a ripped and oversized shirt. In doing so, I proclaimed,

> This tie is a proverbial noose. When I wear this "proper clothing"
> it is a mask for the trauma my body feels. This, this is how I truly
> feel—ripped, ravished, and torn.

This movement, in my eyes, represented the unspoken violence inflicted by the unilinear knowledge and conformity that the space called for. It was a physical manifestation of the ancestral beratement and current day mistreatment of Black physical and intellectual labor. This was a performance. Now on display was my flesh—an undeniable visual that forced us to critically re-examine the engrained and unthought of aspects of the activity. It destabilized the concrete. An equally powerful moment saw Taylor speaking about the expected attitudes of Black women. Mid-sentence, however, I stood up, walked over, and covered her mouth with my hands. I then shouted—"I am the debate space. I will silence you and tell you that you are speaking for yourself." After which, we sat in silence for half a minute, allowing the raw emotion of nothingness to permeate the air.

Still was the room and so too were our voices for far too long.

I began this chapter outlining the one simple truth of policy debate, its team-based structure. I wish to end it calling into question the more complex truths of the activity. We as participants, coaches, and onlookers alike must consider how the system of debate currently rests against Eurocentric, imperial notions of knowledge. More than that though, we must consider how debate can be reformed to account for different types of intelligences, different metrics of value. We must not allow the activity to mold its competitors, but instead allow its competitors to mold the activity. Performance debate is visceral; it allows one to interpret their lived experience against a gradient that has formally denied every aspect of their being. It redefines stability for those students who have oftentimes felt alienated by the concept. It challenges our values, ethics, and organizational formations. Is that not what debate is meant to do? Not only to inform, but to shape? Not only to educate, but to empower?

16.
Ship of Faith

Desiree Hill and Maya McGregory

This chapter provides a glimpse into the world of nontraditional debating. As you read it, please keep in mind several things. First, it is only one example of how a debater may implement a nontraditional approach to debate. Some debaters may present familiar arguments on the assigned debate topic with the only difference being their channel of delivery. Other debaters may completely disengage from the assigned debate topic. Second, this is a combination of original poetry, song, and rap. You will be confronted with offensive language and some rather provocative ideas that could be triggering. In short, the students used language, metaphor, and hyperbole to evoke strong emotions from other debaters and their judges. While that may seem to stand in opposition to the themes we present throughout the text, keep in mind these students chose a controversial presentation to spark a critical examination of society and a deep dive into the feelings, emotions, and injustice faced by millions of people every day. This exposes the listener to their genuine lived experience through rhetoric that creates a visceral reaction. This presentation of their case was not an end point. Rather, it was the start of a conversation.—Shawn F. Briscoe

We debated together in high school for four years in the Saint Louis Urban Debate League. We started like any other novice team, running traditional policy debate affirmative cases, disadvantages, and counterplans. We were "traditional" debaters, until our junior year. Our high school had a Black history program, in which we danced to *Rhythm Nation* by Janet Jackson, along with four other classmates. Our debate coaches saw our performance and were excited at the idea of us incorporating our dance and musical talents into debate. We were skeptical at first because we didn't see anyone else engaging in "nontraditional" debate. We didn't think it would work, but our coaches saw our potential and continued to encourage and teach us even through the backlash we received from judges and other teams.[1] Even though our high school record wasn't impressive and we never got the chance to debate outside of Saint Louis, we decided we would go to the University of Kansas (KU) and continue to debate in our own style.

In August 2019 we went to KU and joined its national award-winning debate team. The resolution for the year was "Resolved: The United States Federal Government should establish a national space policy substantially increasing its international space cooperation with the People's Republic of China and/or the Russian Federation in one or more of the following areas: arms control of space weapons; exchange and management of space situational awareness information; joint human spaceflight for deep space exploration; planetary defense; space traffic management; space-based solar power." We had no idea what our strategy going into the season would be, but we knew we wanted to talk about anti-Blackness and *to perform*. A month later one of our coaches joked, "Well, when I think of planetary destruction, I think about how white people are always destroying shit, so maybe we just get rid of all white people." We chuckled at the joke's absurdity, but that day I (Maya) was sitting in my dorm room listening to music. *On and On* by Erykah Badu came on and there's a line in it where she says, "The mothership can't save you so yo a$$ is gon' get left." Then I remembered the conversation with my coach, and I texted Desiree and said, "We got an aff." One week later, lots of energy drinks, a couple late nights, and a lot of time spent with a thesaurus we came up with this . . .

An aff that would get us solidly identified as a *performance team* for four reasons. First, we incorporated original poetry and rap as evidence, rather than relying on lengthy quotations printed in academic journals and texts. Second, competitive debate traditionally encourages students to roleplay as policymakers by evaluating the resolution as a literal statement to explore through the lens of a problem-solution analysis. We leaned into the metaphor of debate as a game. Specifically, we thought of the resolution as a metaphor and our case as a springboard for examining controversial and relevant issues. Third, we used music and dance to enhance the meaning of our message. Fourth, we challenged the norms, conventions, and rules of the activity. These included things such as how we dressed in competition, speaking during each other's speeches, and somewhat disengaging from the annual debate topic.

To better help you understand what a debate round looked like for us, we annotated the text of our aff in several ways. First, we inserted commentary to help you understand what we did in round, why we chose to do certain things, and generally gave insight into what a typical speech looked like. That commentary is indented and printed *in italics*. Second, Desiree was responsible for delivering our first affirmative constructive or aff; however, there were times during her first speech when we both spoke at the same time. Those portions of the case are printed *in boldface with asterisks around them.* Third, there were times when Maya—the second speaker—was the person who spoke instead of Desiree. Those portions are underlined. Finally, there are places in our case where we identified stage directions, which are [identified with brackets in the text].

As a final reminder, this is only one example of myriad approaches to performance debate. Nontraditional debaters' cases differ greatly in both form *and* content. They may write original poetry to advance their case, they may rap their responses to an opponents' argument, they may read poetry as primary sources on the assigned resolution, and so on. They might present arguments in support of the resolution, or they may challenge the system of the game itself. There is no single description of a performance-based approach to debate. This one used rap, music, and dance to reflect on the state of the world.

Here is our case . . .

[Poem]

> *As with any aff you think through the harms (something*
> *bad you want to fix), inherency (the cause of the harms),*
> *plan (how you intend to fix the problem), and solvency*
> *(an explanation of how your plan fixes the problem). We*
> *constructed this aff the same way. This first poem is the*
> *inherency.*

[Changes—H.E.R (instrumental)]

*This instrumental sounds sincere, tired, almost broken. We
start the timer and let the instrumental play for thirty
seconds. We see judges look up from their flows and just
stare at Desiree with remorseful looks on their faces before
she even says anything. Then Desiree speaks.* [2]

As I lay in bed, my legs start to shake
I go into deep thought about how our humanity has been
    forsaken
Enslaved, shot, lynched, whipped
How much more does it take?

How much does it take for you to realize I'm more than just
    Black?
I have beauty, brains, body
Yet you seem to miss all three
And portray me as a maniac

I watch the news and my people cry
Another Black man shot, goodbye

Some protest, riot, or become an advocate to spread more
    peace
But we don't stand a chance against the police

I watch the news, and what do they say?
"The Black Lives Matter Movement, is the new KKK"
Can't you see? No matter what we do, it seems to fit into a
    category of bullshit.
Why? So they can have a reason to make up for slavery,
    colonization, oh and to name their sons "Dick"

White people try to get rid of us in every possible way
Even if it means f?*k!ng up the world

We're placed in communities with fewer resources
Left and forgotten like they don't hear our Voices

We scream and shout for change
but it's already too late

the ocean starts to hit our homes
The fire gets in our lungs
The heat waves knocks us out
Where do we go?

How do we survive a system, whom suppose to help us, kills
    us instead?
"Change will not come if we wait for some other person or
    if we wait for some time. We are the ones we've been
    waiting for," a wise Black man said
I can't get it out of my head
My sisters and brothers are dead
Because the man in charge don't think that climate could
    put us on our deathbed

We're dying,
Not because of natural causes or health concerns, or some
    kind of accident
But because we're Black
We're fighting for survival because we're under attack

[Dramatic pause.]
The instrumental is still playing.
[Maya gets up from her seat and stands next to Desiree.
We sway to the beat of the instrumental.] Judges bury their
    faces in their flow and competitors vigorously start typing
    away on their laptops and whispering to each other trying
    to come up with a strategy.
[Desiree continues . . .]

Are you angry? Do you need to cry? Do you hate yourself?
    Why?
Why take our culture and pose it as your own?
You're on top but you know you don't belong

You're angry, she is too
Your time is ending. Goodbye you

Here are the harms . . .

[OG Bobby Johnson—Que (instrumental)]

*This instrumental sounds angry and rough. It has a hard bass
    drum, and it has snare drums that sound like machine
    guns going off. It's one of those beats that just hits your
    soul, and you can't help but get amped up.*

She's been watching in silence. . . .
But she got us though
You thought you could defeat her? *Hell no*[3]
She's been waiting
<u>Anxiously anticipating</u>
Get ready

*"Her" is the motherboard, which we talk about later in the
    speech.
Judges bury themselves deeper in their flows*

Now look at them, reinforcing the stereotype of an angry
    Black woman

[We get exceedingly loud.]

But nah N!^^@ we pissed off

*Judges' heads pop up from their flows with fear and
    competitors either gasp or turn away from us awkwardly.*

She's mad

"She" is referring to Black women.
When the badge put me in a cage
<u>Tobby worked for no wage</u>

Black people lashed out in rage
She doesn't understand the hate for a Black mermaid

She's mad
Masta kept me in the field while my skin leaked
Scrapes and bruises covered my feet
Because whitey said ³/₅ of me wasn't complete
Masta looked at my body like it was a piece of meat

She's mad
They want to control the traffic in Mars
While they keep us behind bars
They can't even resist pulling me over when my Black a$$
    driving a car

She's mad
I tried to empower my people and they said All lives matter
They rejected my face but loved when Kylie made her lips
    fatter
They try to be "neutral" like blackness is never a factor
Think they can say the n-word just because they listen to,
    insert Black rapper

She's mad
White people are the cause of planetary destruction
Trying to kill us so there won't be any Black reproduction
Talk about reconstruction but it still ain't no justice
Forcing n!**@s out they country, n!**@ that's abduction

She's mad
It's all because Jim tried to control the crows
Billy tried to straighten my fro
Miley thought her ass was Black enough to throw
She sees and she can't take it no mo

She's mad
Give them space weapons and they might try to kill us in
    space

<u>Might try to leave our bodies up there without a trace</u>
Devalued because of my race
<u>Yelled at and spat on like imma disgrace</u>

She's mad
The government tryna be space aware
<u>B!+%h do it look like I care</u>
I got sick and the doctor denied my healthcare
<u>Can't run to another country because anti-Black people are</u>
   everywhere

She's mad
And she has the right to be
<u>She has 18 years of anger to talk about in a 9-minute speech</u>
The only time there's Black cooperation is when negativity is
   involved
<u>Putting up borders so we won't evolve</u>
Then try to cooperate like things are resolved.
<u>But nah</u>

She's mad
<u>She's tired</u>
She's angry
She can't take it no mo,

The instrumental goes off
We have a Dialogue . . . a Discussion

What is there left to do?
<u>Riot?</u> Nah, can't be too violent
<u>Protest?</u> Nah, did that. Still no respect
<u>Shoot them?</u> Nah, we don't wanna make a mess
<u>Ship them to another continent?</u> Nah that's not good
   enough, they're everywhere: China, Russia, India too. We
   gotta think of something better to do.
<u>Maybe send them to space?</u>
gasp
yeaaaaaaaaaaaaaaaaaaaaaaaaaaaaaaaaaaaaaaaaaaaaaaaaaaaaa

This is the plan. . . .

The United States federal government, the Russian
     federation and the Peoples Republic of China
     should cooperate by strapping anti-Black whites to
     motherboards and sending them on a one-way trip to
     space to deflect asteroids.[4]

. . . .

[song starts]

ship of faith, ship of faith
OOOooo
ship of faith, ship of faith
Only thing to do is send them to their doom
ship of faith, ship of faith, ship of faith, ship of faith
Only thing to do is send them to their doom
ship of faith, ship of faith, ship of faith, of faith

*This is a parody from the song "Over The Moon" from our
     favorite musical, Rent. We simply added this part just
     because it sounded cool. We don't think many people got
     the reference though. Lol.*

[calls motherboard]

*[Desiree uses her hand as an imaginary phone to make a call
     to the motherboard]*

[phone rings]

[The imaginary phone rings and she picks up.]

Hello? Yes motherboard we're ready. Pull up

This is the solvency. . . .

[B* From The South—Mulatto (instrumental)]

*This instrumental sounds energetic. It starts off with a beat
that sounds like a trash truck backing up, so it is perfect
to create the image in the judge's head that a vehicle is
moving. In our case we wanted them to picture a big,
galactic spaceship. That's how we picture the motherboard.*

*[We start dancing around the room, twerking on desks,
throwing cash, and singing this. . . .]*

[Chorus]

We about to send you to space
We about to e-rase yo race[5]
You about to get sent to yo doom[6]
Motherboard about to go vroom
You about to get sent to yo doom
Motherboard about to go vroom

*While reading the chorus, it is important to note that we
did not really advocate for elimination or removal of any
group of people. Ultimately, we used our coach's absurd
statement as a way of forcing a difficult conversation on
and an examination of race and racism in our society.[7]*

*[Desiree starts rapping, Maya keeps dancing and adding
adlibs.]*

*Some people bop their heads to the beat and smile, and others
hide behind their laptops. Either way, we keep our energy
up.*

[Verse 1]

Who the f&*k got shot this time
White folks killing my mind this time
They say he had a strap,[8] they lying
Now they got my n!**@s . . . f&*k!ng crying

B!+*h Im mad

They don't apologize
They just monetize
Fill me with lies
Like paper could make the mental greater
When it can't cause they just do it later

Stop and frisk was created for my n!**@s
To multiply the cells with color
No division

Now listen

[**Repeat Chorus**]

We're not putting up with it, we're done
She coming strapped
We ain't talking 'bout guns
We talking chains,
to put you in yo lane
No more of the fame
And you're the one to blame

This is not a game
We are not clowns
***You know what it is when H&M** [our team code was
    Kansas HM] **come around***
So sit the f^#k down and just wait
She coming real soon
to take you out this place

[**Bridge**]

Start up the engine
You 'bout to go missing
See you from a distance
We ain't tryna listen
Bout to erase, racists from the earth

Come on, my n!**@s let's get them off our turf [*the beat
    plays and we dance*] (x2)
I said, come on, my n!**@s let's get them off our turf cause . . .

[Repeat Chorus]

> *After the speech is over and the timer goes off, we stand next
> to each other and glance at our competitors, waiting for
> them to start the timer for cross-examination. Some seem
> flustered, some seem arrogant, either way, we stay in
> "performance mode"; every question is answered with a line
> in the speech, a dance, a laugh, or a petty remark. We set a
> fun, somewhat humorous mood for the rest of the round.*

The poetry and rap song we wrote for this speech represents a pivotal moment not only in our debate careers but also in our lives. When we started to
do *performance debate* in high school, we continuously met negativity from
judges, coaches, and competitors. Thanks to the love and support from our
coaches we persevered and were blessed enough to continue our partnership
on one of the best college debate teams in the nation. We made it to elimination rounds at every tournament we attended and won multiple speaker
awards. Not only were we succeeding statistically, but we were also creating
a name for ourselves in the college debate community. Judges would walk
in the room and get excited when they saw us because they knew watching
us would be a fun experience. We were succeeding in debate with our own
art, our own vernacular, and our own style.

That was empowering. It made us realize that if none of our plans work
out, we can try being a rap duo because we got bars; we are pretty good at
debate, despite how many ballots we lost in high school; and *we are enough*.
We thought we had to read at supersonic speed and have the neatest flows to
be good at debate, but we realized that we don't have to conform to be successful. We learned through this experience that we are capable of greatness
with the intelligence, skills, and talents that we already possess, no matter
how unconventional or abnormal they may seem.

Notes

1. Examples of backlash from judges in our league included: "your aff
have no structure," "add cards," ignoring the entirety of the performance

because it was not "traditional," "too much cursing," "dancing and singing does not bring about real world change," "the performance contributed to unneeded stereotypes placed on African Americans," "More textual evidence was definitely needed, though I do not believe it will actually help this case."

2. Almost the entire case is original poetry written by us.

3. Some of the rules, norms, and conventions we broke included speaking during each other's speeches. As a reminder, we say the *boldface text with asterisks* together. Maya, as the second speaker, interjects with the underlined text.

4. Our plan was a metaphorical statement designed to connect our arguments to the annual debate topic and establish a hypothetical image of a world in which anti-Black whites no longer hold power.

5. *Editor's note*: I struggled deeply with whether or not rhetoric such as this has a place in society generally and academia specifically. The words used are harsh and hateful. However, the authors explained that there are multiple contexts at play that should point to a nonliteral interpretation. They asserted that the lines in question were rhetorical and lyrical devices intended to advance a needed conversation. Having worked with the authors, knowing their coaches in high school, and having had a discussion with them about the chapter, their intentions seemed good and hopeful rather than harsh and hateful. Nevertheless, I could write an entire chapter, if not an entire book, on my conflicting thoughts about the line and the broader context they provided me. Perhaps that is the point.

6. *Editor's note*: This performance, or nontraditional approach to debate, was an original work of music by the authors. While the lyrics may seem out of place in an academic work or in an academic setting, it is important to remember that the authors were using a different channel of communication to share their thoughts, feelings, emotions, and knowledge. It is not uncommon for artists to use rhetoric that is shocking, not meant to be taken literally, metaphorical, pushing boundaries, and so forth to convey a message. Note that at points where the authors' lyrics are the most questionable, they referenced that their opponents and judges frequently started smiling, swaying, or moving along with the music. It seems their delivery enabled their opponents to recognize that they were not in actuality spreading messages of hate.

Here are a handful of songs from pop culture, spanning decades and genres, that took similar liberties with their lyrics. "Run for Your Life" by the Beatles: "I'd rather see you dead, little girl. Than to be with another man . . . You'd better run for your life if you can." "Baby, Let's Play House" by Elvis: "Try to understand. I'd rather see you dead, little girl. Than to be with another man." "Delilah" by Tom Jones: "She stood there laughing. I felt the knife in my hand and she laughed no more." "Folsom Prison Blues" by Johnny Cash: "I shot a man in Reno just to watch him die." "Pumped Up Kicks" by Foster the People: "All the other kids with the pumped-up kicks. You better run; better run outrun my gun." "L.A. County" by Lyle Lovett: "I just stood there watching. As that .45 told them goodbye." "Ruby Don't Take Your Love to Town" by Kenny Rogers: "And if I could move I'd get my gun and put her in the ground." "Knoxville Girl" by the Louvin Brothers: "She never spoke another word, I only beat her more, Until the ground around me within her blood did flow." "Dancing in the Dark" by Bruce Springsteen: "This gun's for hire." "Goodbye Earl" by the Chicks: lyrics and a music video about killing a domestic abuser. "Martha Divine" by Ashley McBryde: "Your ass is mine. And it ain't murder if I bury you alive." "I Shot the Sheriff" by Bob Marley and the Wailers: See title. "Used to Lover Her" by Guns N' Roses: "I used to love her, but I had to kill her . . . She's buried right in my back-yard." "Bohemian Rhapsody" by Queen: "Mama, just killed a man. Put a gun against his head, pulled the trigger, now he's dead." "Bombtrack" by Rage Against the Machine: "Dispute the suits, I ignite, and then watch 'em burn. Burn burn, yes, you're gonna burn!" "Down with the Sickness" by Disturbed: "How would you like to see how it feels Mommy? Here it comes, get ready to die." "Burn It Down" by Linkin Park: "We can't wait to burn it to the ground." "Bodies" by Drowning Pool: "Let the bodies hit the floor." "Damage, Inc." by Metallica: "Victim is your name, and you shall fall. Blood will follow blood. Dying time is here."

This list could go on for pages. Rightly or wrongly, it appears music is a location where rhetoric is sometimes used in ways that are not literal. Thus, the message must be uncovered through careful consideration of the multiple contexts surrounding the performance.

7. *Editor's note*: Finally, the authors presented this in an academic, competitive environment. Thus, their statements, rhetoric, and perceived advocacies were open to interrogation and debate, meaning they had to justify and defend them based upon the critiques of their opponents and judges. Not only did they have to defend their arguments regarding the injustice present in society and whether the debate tournament was an appropriate time and place for that to happen, they also had to defend their rhetoric, presentation, use of metaphor, use of music, and advocacies (perceived or actual).

8. Strap is slang for gun.

17.
A Tool for Career Readiness

Ravi Rao

I debated for four years in a traditional, suburban circuit that eschewed the more technical, rapid-fire style of policy debate in favor of something more oratorical. Our version of debate was what the average layperson might expect: high school students decked out in suits, speaking passionately about government policy in a style designed to be accessible. I then debated policy in college for roughly two years, trying rather unsuccessfully to adapt to the rapid-fire delivery and more nuanced, technical strategies popular in that circuit. I also debated in the more oratorical parliamentary format, at a time when it was just emerging as a popular alternative to policy debate on the collegiate level.

In the late 1990s, a group of universities and philanthropies began a concerted effort to promote debate in urban public schools. This urban debate movement saw nascent *urban debate leagues* sprout up in places like New York City, Atlanta, Chicago, Saint Louis, and Kansas City. I was part of that first cohort of college debaters hired by these emerging urban debate leagues to teach debate to urban high school students. The resultant influx of students from urban schools into the broader debate community would, over the ensuing decades, lead to the emergence of a third style of policy debate: *performance debate*, with its focus on personal identity, structural power dynamics, and critical theory.

After briefly flirting with a legal career, I found myself coaching in the second wave of urban debate, as the founding executive director of the Saint Louis Urban Debate League and, later, as a debate coach at Lindenwood University. While I am a firm believer in the merits of all three approaches to policy debate—traditional, technical, performance—my experience coaching the performance style, my side hustle as an (employment) interview coach, and my work with a nonprofit that teaches job skills, have led me to conclude that performance debate is an excellent career preparation tool that all high schools and colleges should actively promote.

What Is Performance Debate?

There is no shortage of authors who can better describe what performance debate is. The aspect of performance I want to stress is that relative to the traditional and technical forms of debate, *performance debate* emphasizes the intersections between a debater's personal identity and the debate topic or the norms of debate as practiced.

Broadly speaking, a traditional debater might argue that lowering restrictions on immigration would help the U.S. economy. A more technical debater might argue that lowering restrictions on a specific class of work visas would help the U.S. economy by diversifying the labor pool, increasing innovation, and improving trade relations. A performance debater, however, might argue that their own personal experience as the child of immigrants should not only impact the discussion, but is also a prerequisite to formulating a meaningful understanding of how immigration policy affects real people. While traditional and technical debate are grounded in a macro, top-down worldview, *performance* often centers the debate on the individuals in the room. Performance debate is much more personal; it turns the identity of the debater into grounds for an argument.

Know Your Story

If performance debate concerns the intersections between personal identities, the norms of the debate activity, and accessing the levers of policymaking power in society, then preparation begins with an examination of personal identity. As a coach, I ask my debaters to begin by exploring who they are: both their social location and personal interests.

Social location refers to the groups people belong to because of their position in society—defined by gender, race, social class, age, ability, religion, sexual orientation, cultural heritage, and geographic location. The theory is that two people from different social locations experience the world in different ways. (*For example, a white student might find the dread an Asian student feels over earning a B on an assignment incomprehensible.*) A true mutual understanding occurs only after they begin by recognizing the differences in their social locations. (*The two students above might compare how their parents may react differently to the aforementioned B, including by questioning the very stereotype by which I posited that the Asian student might feel more dread.*) Once a debater identifies their social location, they must examine how that social location intersects with policymaking/decision-making power and/or debating. How does my identity as an Asian male impact the way I view a debate topic on drug addiction?

It is important to warn students before they engage in performance debate that this is the most personally difficult, emotionally taxing style of debate. Since a debater's own identity and personal story become part of the argument, they become grounds for opposition. This can be traumatizing for a student who has not prepared themselves emotionally for this inevitability. I have seen debaters have their stated gender identity questioned, their commitment to diversity openly ridiculed, or their vulnerabilities in discussing sexual violence exploited in a bout of victim-blaming. While it is liberatory for students to stand up for themselves and advocate for people like them, it also makes them incredibly vulnerable. Thus, the practice may not be for everybody, and coaching teams through these emotional minefields is certainly labor intensive.

Once a debater identifies the aspects of their social location they wish to explore and determines to engage in this personal form of debate, I ask them to explore their personal interests. I refer to those interests, likes, and desires that make up each person's unique individuality. How does each student prefer to express themselves, and can we build arguments around those modes of expression? I coached or evaluated teams that expressed themselves by reading fables, drawing pictograms, reading original poetry, playing scenes from movies, and/or dancing in their debate rounds. Teams then used those modes of communication to craft a case, a compelling work of performance art designed to elicit both rational and emotional agreements with whatever their central argument was.

The point isn't whether these are *"good" arguments* or even *winning arguments*—others can certainly engage in that debate. My point is merely that engaging in the practice of *performance debate* forces the debater to engage in their own personal story; to figure out who they are in terms of their group identities or personal interests, and how each of those might intersect policymaking and/or political expression. How does your gender identity or sexual orientation inform how you view the world? How you view policy? How policy affects you? How you view policy debate as an educational activity? How your participation in policy debate and the educational system affects you? How does your race or cultural upbringing impact your ability to navigate political questions as an adult? These questions are fundamental to our identities as political beings, and yet nowhere else in a liberal education are we asked to tackle them.

Your Story Matters

There is an intrinsic value to knowing your own story, beyond just the development of political beings. Folks in public relations speak of *controlling the narrative*, and in the political media it is often referred to as *spin*. That same principle applies to students as they transition into the working world: they must sell themselves to employers. Those who *control the narrative* and apply the right *spin* have a distinct advantage in the job market. I opened this chapter with a recitation of my own story, and it is one I have told quite a few times. I am familiar with my own story because I practiced telling it in job interview after job interview, which led me to my side gig as an interview coach.

Job Interviews for Dummies

I used to think that, as a debater, I would be naturally adept at handling job interviews. Then a senior partner at a prestigious regional law firm asked the twenty-two-year-old version of me what my greatest weakness was.

Hardly a difficult question, nor one that should catch you by surprise. But when you are applying to clerk at a law firm that can basically put you straight through law school and into a career-track position and have the privilege of interviewing before a senior partner, you should hope to have enough sense to not answer "getting out of bed." As someone who was dealing with a chronically undermedicated, severe case of depression, my answer was as honest as it was damning. Nobody ever coached me on interviewing, so I simply did not realize he was expecting me to *spin* that personal weakness into a story of learning, personal growth, or perseverance.

As a side hustle, I work with American and immigrant first-generation college students to teach them the interview skills I presume the rest of you get from your professional parents or family members. While my practice revolves primarily around interviewing, it includes networking and soft skills many immigrants simply never had to practice or learn prior to coming here. In that work, I focus on three truths I learned from my own experience, and honed by working with performance debaters:

1. How you portray your experience matters more than the experience itself. People care more about the details of the experience (*what did you learn, how many contracts did you execute, how many accounts did you handle*) than the fact that you spent two versus four years at it. I coach my clients to be specific in their details, use round numbers so they don't get tripped up, and try to circle those details back to the qualifications in a job posting. In performance debate, students often write their narratives with an eye for specific, memorable details that draw the audience's attention, and try to frame their experience to match what is in a particular piece of supporting textual evidence.

2. Each question is an opportunity, even if it asks about a negative. "My greatest weakness" is a chance to tell the tale of "how I overcame my greatest weakness." "My worst personality trait" is a chance to demonstrate that "I practice regular, honest self-reflection, and work on self-improvement." Clients should make a list of all the interview questions they have been asked (or their peers were asked for similar jobs, or they have heard an employer likes to ask) and prepare stock anecdotes for each. Performance debaters make lists of all the arguments they hear, and spend days before each competition brainstorming, researching, and crafting compelling answers to each (many of which are equally as artistic as the original case elements).

3. Practice makes perfect. I have friends who apply and interview for jobs they have zero interest in taking, just to practice interviewing in a setting that counts. While I do not go that far, interviewing is a skill like anything else. Performance debaters are always practicing their performances—not just in practice debates, but at open mic nights, talent shows, etc.

Performance Debate Practitioners Develop Emotional Intelligence

Charles DeLeón, a law student at the University of the District of Columbia David A. Clark School of Law, was one of the first debaters I coached in college. He notes that his "experience as a debater benefitted from an infusion of his cultural values, and beliefs." On a military intervention topic, Charles argued that a lack of genuine cultural understanding through indigenous knowledge would always lead to intervening forces being viewed as hostile occupiers. To illustrate this, he read fables about predatory animals. This argument was not the most competitively successful strategy, but it was one that paid homage to Charles's cultural roots. "This infusion made it easier to be visible in a world that looked to make me invisible by any means necessary."

Competitive debate tends to favor scholarly evidence produced by academics. Rather than reproduce that scholarship in his debates, and do what so many other debaters did, reading fables and even his own original Spanish poetry in debates gave Charles a unique method of engagement. By using the platform debate afforded him to explore his roots while educating others, Charles gained confidence as an advocate for issues that mattered to him, and the emotional intelligence to navigate potential fallout.

"Particularly because of debate and the critical skills I gained from it, I have become highly involved in activism and it has created the fluidity I required to move around in a society that tries to keep people in boxes." Debate taught Charles to read his audiences, tailor his presentation depending on the level of hostility or amenability he perceived, but to nevertheless keep advocating for what he believed in. As a current law student, Charles describes his progression: "I now advocate for full liberation, through learning theory, and then applying the theory into praxis. [My experience] has cultivated me as an individual that I hold in high regard and love deeply."

Emotional Intelligence Is a Job Skill

Many human resource professionals note the importance of emotional intelligence as a highly sought-after job skill. According to the World Economic Forum's Future of Jobs Report, emotional intelligence will be one of the top ten job skills in 2020 and beyond.[1] As technological advances in artificial intelligence, machine learning, advanced robotics, autonomous transportation, and genomics change the way we live and work, many jobs will disappear, while other new jobs that do not exist today will emerge. So, while negotiation and active listening were seen as top ten job skills for 2015, both are expected to drop from the top ten as machines, using masses of data, begin to make decisions for us.[2] Navigating these changes will require emotional intelligence from all of us, catapulting it onto the list for the first time.[3]

Emotional intelligence is the ability to process emotions, control your responses, and make sound decisions.[4] Experts say the ability to both identify and name your own emotions, the ability to harness those emotions and apply them, and the ability to manage emotions (including self-regulation and helping others to do the same) will greatly increase your chances for success in the workplace.

Emotional intelligence is of growing importance as the expectation for large change increases. Hiring managers increasingly value emotional intelligence because "dealing with workplace pressures and functioning well under stress demands an ability to manage our emotions."[5] Thus, as technology is expected to dramatically change the way we work (we need look no further than the explosion of video conferencing and network infrastructures, as the global pandemic of 2020 pushed many employers to offer remote work-from-home options), employers will increasingly value those employees who can manage their stress levels.[6]

Employers also value emotional intelligence because people who have high levels of emotional intelligence tend to understand well and cooperate better with others, especially across different cultures and backgrounds. In an increasingly diversifying, globalized workplace, the ability to recognize emotions and regulate emotional responses will be even more important.[7] Similarly, high emotional intelligence is viewed by employers as correlating with being a good listener, being more open to feedback, being more empathetic, setting a better example for others to follow, and making more thoughtful and thorough decisions.[8] Workplace training vendor

TalentSmart estimates that emotional intelligence is responsible for as much as 58 percent of your job performance.[9]

Performance Debate Replicates the Process of Developing Emotional Intelligence

Emotional intelligence, unlike intelligence, is developed relatively easily.[10] There are four qualities highly associated with emotional intelligence that people can develop through practice, either by themselves or with a personal coach.[11] Among debate styles, performance debate is uniquely positioned to develop each of these qualities.

First, emotional intelligence requires people to *know themselves*.[12] This comes as part of an ongoing, reflective process, in which clients consider what their emotional strengths and weaknesses are, how their current mood affects their thoughts and decision-making, and what is happening under the surface that influences what others say or do?[13] Similarly, performance debate requires debaters to first consider the emotional fallout and/or risks they will undertake by sharing personal experiences publicly, before identifying what aspects of their stories they will craft into the performance.

Second, emotional intelligence requires the ability to *read other people's emotions*.[14] Empathy and compassion—the ability to understand, share, and have concern for the feelings of another—are directly connected to emotional intelligence. Can you understand another person's thought process even if you disagree with it; can you listen without judging?[15] Performance debate requires participants to be aware of the emotional states of the judge and other competitors, to determine how moving the performance is and adjust accordingly. The most successful performance debaters can identify and respond to emotional responses to their arguments in a way that more logic-driven debate practitioners struggle with.

Third, emotional intelligence involves *choosing how to express your own feelings*.[16] Emotional intelligence isn't the ability to self-regulate what emotions you feel, but rather how you react to them in choosing to express yourself. Similarly, performance debaters must constantly practice self-regulation in debates as elements of their personal story get called into question or otherwise treated adversely. If I were arguing that my identity as an Asian male has subjected me to racial violence, an opponent might call that into question by pointing out that Asian Americans tend to score well on various socioeconomic factors (education level, earning potential, etc.), and that this outweighs the slight risk of racial violence. While my temptation might be to get defensive, a more successful approach would be to self-regulate my emotional reaction, and instead calmly point out that socioeconomic status did not insulate me from racial violence, and does not protect other Asian Americans, either.

Finally, emotional intelligence involves the *freedom to adapt*.[17] Hiring managers increasingly look for candidates who are adaptable—who can pivot and flourish amidst rapid change. All debaters practice *judge adaptation*: the ability to adapt your argument and style to appeal to the individual(s) judging the debate. At a debate tournament, students typically compete in four, six, or eight consecutive debates. They might have a layperson judging one debate, a college debater judging another debate, and a public speaking coach judging yet another debate. Each require different adaptations: the layperson will most likely react adversely to jargon and fast delivery. The college debater will likely appreciate more nuance and is more likely to find jargon and rapid delivery acceptable. The public speaking coach may appreciate some nuance but will shun rapid delivery.

Performance debaters have yet another wrinkle to manage. In addition to navigating the layperson, debater, and coach archetypes, performance debaters must ascertain a judge's receptivity to performance/identity arguments. As the newest style of debate, performance debating is not as widely acceptable as the technical or traditional variants—and many judges may be predisposed for or against such modes of debating. Still, the best performance debaters manage to adapt their presentation to appeal to a wide variety of judges.

Performance Debate Prepares Students for Job Interviews

Your story is more than just something to debate about. A job interview is, essentially, a chance to share selections from your story. Coaches who prepare clients for job interviews use storytelling as a part of their practice.

Employment Connection is a forty-year-old nonprofit organization in Saint Louis, Missouri, that is dedicated to removing barriers that prevent people from achieving self-sufficiency through employment.[18] Its signature program, a job readiness training called World of Work, teaches participants basic skills for the job search: how to fill out an application, how to write a resume, what to wear for interviews, how to prepare for interviews, and so forth. After the twenty-four-hour, three-day course, participants are paired with a career specialist who supports them through their job hunt.

One major reason the World of Work program is so successful is that it emphasizes developing the proper mindset, especially for job interviews. "We work hard to instill the confidence and skills that our clients need to excel when they participate in employment interviews. We reinforce that they have the talent, passion and abilities to make a successful contribution to the position they are seeking," says Sal Martinez, CEO of Employment Connection. The way career specialists do this is to take inventory of each client's experiences, strengths, and weaknesses, and then practice crafting those components into interview responses.

Darron Collins-Bey is the manager of Out of School Youth Programs at Employment Connection, and a former career specialist. In his experience conducting mock interviews, the most crucial part of preparing clients for the interview boils down to establishing a connection. "We teach them that everything they need to be successful; they already have in their minds. They need to form a connection with whomever is interviewing them—and that means being relatable, being able to find something in common. They need to present what's on [their resume] in a positive light that makes the [interviewer] want to hire them. We help them tell their story in a way that frames the narrative in a positive light." Beyond framing the narrative, storytelling can play a role in establishing a connection with the interviewer: "Say you notice that the interviewer has a framed photo of [Saint Louis Cardinals legend] Ozzie Smith on the wall, you might break the ice with a story about how you met Ozzie, or how you got to see him play, or even just that you used to play ball. Something that connects you to the interviewer."

In my own practice as an interview coach, I encourage clients to identify experiences that fit several *typical* job interview questions: what is your greatest strength/weakness, what is a mistake you made that you learned from, why do you want this job, etc. Rather than providing straightforward answers (*"I struggle to get out of bed"*), I want clients to relate experiences that demonstrate a clear progression (*"I used to struggle to get out of bed, until [some experience happened] and I learned to motivate myself by pursuing personally meaningful work, such as [that which you do here]."*) Once clients identify the experiences that fit each question type, they must craft an anecdote around it, and then practice delivering it in an interview setting. It is no coincidence that I coach my performance debaters in exactly the same way: first, they must identify personal experiences that relate to the debate topic, then craft some form of performance around it (a narrative, poetry, choreographed dance, etc.), and finally practice performing it.

Conclusion

All forms of debate are worthwhile as career preparation. They all develop communication and advocacy skills that are invaluable in the workplace and do so at a level superior to many other academic activities. That said, performance debate is uniquely situated to develop a participant's self-knowledge, emotional awareness, ability to self-regulate, and adaptability in ways that less personal modes of debate do not. As a debate coach with experience in several styles of debate, I can attest to how performance debate uniquely develops emotional intelligence. As an interview coach, I can attest to how important it is for candidates to be able to tell stories that are both relatable and relevant.

If the COVID-19 pandemic taught us anything, it is that adaptability is crucial to continued success. Very few activities develop adaptability and agility like debate, and very few styles of debate develop adaptability like performance debate.

Notes

1. Alex Gray, "The 10 Skills You Need to Thrive in the Fourth Industrial Revolution," *World Economic Forum*, January 19, 2016, accessed January 21, 2021, https://www.weforum.org/agenda/2016/01/the-10-skills-you-need-to-thrive-in-the-fourth-industrial-revolution/.

2. Gray.

3. Gray.

4. Zornista Licheva, "Why Emotional Intelligence Is a Top 10 Skill," *Access MBA*, February 21, 2020, accessed January 21, 2021, https://www.accessmba.com/articles/view/why-emotional-intelligence-is-a-top-10-skill.

5. Harvey Deutschendorf, "7 Reasons Why Emotional Intelligence Is One of the Fastest-Growing Job Skills," *Fast Company*, May 4, 2016, accessed January 21, 2021, https://www.fastcompany.com/3059481/7-reasons-why-emotional-intelligence-is-one-of-the-fastest-growing-job-skills#:~:text=According%20to%20the%20World%20Economic,been%20growing%20in%20recent%20years.

6. Deutschendorf.

7. Deutschendorf.

8. Deutschendorf.

9. "Homepage," TalentSmartEQ, 2020, accessed February 6, 2021, https:://www.talentsmarteq.com.

10. Licheva.

11. Licheva.

12. Licheva.

13. Licheva.

14. Licheva.

15. Licheva.

16. Licheva.

17. Licheva.

18. "Homepage," Employment Connection, 2020, accessed June 23, 2021, https://www.employmentstl.org/.

Section Five
Power in Our Voices

I'm a true master you can check my credentials
'Cause I choose to use my infinite potential
                    "Come Clean," Jeru the Damaja

By now, it should be clear that academic debate—regardless of the form taken—is a unique activity. From the audience-friendly perspectives of traditional competitive circuits to the rapid-fire and jargon-laced delivery of progressive circuits to the nontraditional and varied approaches of diverse students, debate connects to nearly every facet of life.

One of the unique aspects of academic debate is that it is not reliant upon teachers sharing insights with students, directing the transfer of knowledge into empty vessels, nor dictating how and what is discussed by those in the classroom. Rather, debate offers frameworks for understanding the world around us. It makes space for students to work out the content using those structures as a guide in their academic and competitive pursuits.

Does it help uncover truth? Does it help build meaningful relationships? Does it help us understand others? Does it help us in our careers? Does it uncover its own limitations? Does it reveal flaws in our educational system? Does it illuminate possible pathways forward? Does it help us make the world a better place? In a word—*Yes.*

Much debate within the community exists over a philosophical question regarding whether the activity empowers students. Does it unlock voices, or does it merely showcase the intellect and power of voices that already existed? To me, this is a largely irrelevant question. Both are true. Debate is something that matters, and we should invest in it, and correspondingly, in our students.

18.
In It Together

Nicole Wanzer-Serrano

Driving around my neighborhood in 2020, I saw signs that proudly proclaimed, "In it together." I physically couldn't stop myself from shaking my head. How could we be *in it together* to stop COVID, but not to stop cycles of poverty that existed five minutes away? How could we be *in it together* to save lives from COVID, but not to save lives lost through racism? How could we be *in it together* to respect six-feet distancing, but not to respect someone's pronouns? It was easy to call out the hypocrisy of these signs from the comfort of my car. A year later and it doesn't feel like we are *in it together*. While the world embraced *social distancing*, the many small cracks in our world seemed to deepen. Little boxes of faces on a computer fighting for speaking time in meetings. Social media newsfeeds that become silent shouting matches over how the world is and should be. Whether *unfriending* someone on social media or refusing to engage in conversations, it feels like the world is more divided than ever. Although removing toxicity and conserving your energy is important, our world moves forward by joint effort. The global pandemic has reemphasized that our world is interconnected. For our society to move forward, we really need everyone to be *in it together* against the greatest problems of our times.

How then do we truly live the ethic of *in it together*? What is the next step after putting up the sign in your front yard? This book gives you a powerful answer: debate. Encourage each young person to participate in interscholastic speech and debate. Make sure this generation has the skills that come from being part of a speech and debate team and that they understand how to use these skills to the ends of humility, equity, integrity, leadership, respect, and service. Debate can teach young people how to be critically self-reflective. Debate can create lifelong learners. Debate can show students the power of their voices to create the change they want in *their* world.

Because it has a particular resolution that students discuss, debate creates the opportunity for perspective taking. Whether through assigned advocacy or through the nature of refuting your opponents' arguments, young people explore myriad perspectives from round to round.

Like a diamond in the rough, as more pressure is put on the issue, a more multifaceted diamond appears. Each perspective creates another face on our always refining diamond. Encouraging and entertaining more perspectives on an issue allows us to see the light and the way forward in our world. Debate, at its best, is not about forcing students to choose one side over another on an issue, but instead about encouraging students to explore and understand the myriad perspectives.

After their time in debate is completed, perspective taking has taught young people to understand the many ways to tackle any number of issues from climate change to education reform. More fundamentally, perspective taking teaches students empathy. Debate creates a space where students' biases or assumptions are confronted, where they are encouraged to listen actively, and most importantly understand the other team. As debate has expanded to include more personal experiences and new forms of argumentation—like those discussed by Nic Nave, Jamal Burns, Maya McGregory, and Desiree Hill—the ability for students to learn empathy has expanded. It is impossible to expect all young people to have shared the same experiences. Interscholastic debate offers the *best opportunity* to teach our students how to sympathize and empathize with others; how to understand not just their opinions, but also the logic and assumptions used to reach those opinions.

Debate in any form encourages research and critical thinking. The longer a topic is a question for competition and the deeper a student commits to that area, the more that research and reflection occurs. With a year-long topic for policy debate, students learn about a breadth of issues. To a casual spectator, it may appear young people are running to extremes or exploring ideas that are only tangentially related to the topic. Instead, these students are understanding that the world is interconnected and complex. Students learn that policy decisions shouldn't be evaluated in the vacuum of the halls of Congress nor through the myopic view of a single issue, but instead should reflect the many ways in which those decisions impact the lives of people. Furthermore, the longer students participate in interscholastic debate, the more the activity encourages them to anticipate and prepare for opposing viewpoints.

Whether it is last-minute research between competition or long days in a library, young people learn to explore topics they are passionate about and for which others are passionate. It is in the moments when debate encourages a student to pick up yet *another* book on environmental justice or read yet *another* article on carbon sequestration that debate creates lifelong learners. Stories like that of Ashley Snooke's debate background sparking her interest in foreign policy and international relations, laying a foundation for a career that spanned the globe are not an anomaly within this activity.

In my career, I have met a lot of speech and debate alums. I also meet a lot of partners and family members of alums. Inevitably, the family member shares a story of seeing this alum discover an area of passion and researching it to extreme levels of minutia. Pursuing the perceived extremes of an area also moves societal conversations forward. My husband, a former debater, discovered his passion while working on his PhD. He literally wrote the book on the New York chapter of the Young Lords, a group that fought for neighborhood empowerment, social justice, and revolutionary change for Puerto Ricans, Latina/o/x folks more broadly, and other colonized peoples. When he first learned of the Young Lords, his studies would have been considered exploring an area not in the mainstream or core of communications studies. His ability to follow his passion and apply his research skills moved the conversation forward. This boundary pushing in debate also teaches young people to understand that as we learn more, the truth changes. Like the proverbial elephant in a dark room, as you discover more information, you get a better idea of what animal is standing next to you. Debate teaches young people that an absolute truth or absolute winning argument does not exist. Instead, we make the best choices we can with the best information available; then, we immediately start preparing ourselves for the next decision point.

Debate also prepares young people for moments of crisis, like Tara Tate spoke about with her daughter's NICU journey. My son CJ was also a micro preemie, born at twenty-four weeks gestationally and weighing under a pound. We almost lost him a few times and had to suddenly become experts on how to parent a medically fragile child. Two years later, pregnant with my daughter, I attended the University of Iowa Stead Family Children's Hospital Conference on the care of periviable infants to better understand how they saved my son's life. One of my son's neonatologists presented research findings that emphasized just how thankful I should be that my child was alive. The research findings also showed that one of the key factors in a child, like CJ, surviving and thriving is if they have a "better" parent. They defined *better parents* as those who educate themselves on what's happening, engage in the care process, and effectively advocate for their child. I couldn't better encapsulate what years of debate camp and tournaments taught me than that list. I knew how to ask questions and process volumes of information quickly. I knew how to decipher *expertise*, but still look for opposing viewpoints. I never liked medicine, but I learned the skills needed to delve into and understand new subjects because it was important to the moment and my goal. I am writing here because at my core I believe that my and my husband's speech and debate experience helped save my son's life.

Debate is so much more than just an academic pursuit of your passions or preparing for decisions. The interscholastic activity of debate has a beautiful element of set time constraints so young people learn to speak, to listen, and to question each other. Fear of public speaking is common. Debate, at its best, creates a space where a timid student has something to say. As a coach and as an executive director, I saw countless students tell me they were too scared to speak. In the context of a practice round, and then later a beginning competition round, I saw these same students slowly become more comfortable speaking. Novice debate tournaments were my *favorite* experience as an executive director. In the morning, rounds end in just a few minutes because the students can barely fill up a minute or two of reading their cases. By the afternoon, these young people are arguing with judges about why they should have won!

My first year as the executive director of the Dallas Urban Debate Alliance, I created a video to thank some of our donors by interviewing a few students who had won awards that semester. Jon[1] was a senior at a high school with a newer team. Jon told me he joined debate because a guidance counselor placed him in the debate class to fill up his schedule. He told me school was not "his thing." In fact, the year before, he had been in one of the alternative district schools, but he figured he'd get an easy A in the class by going to one Saturday tournament with a friend. Jon was shocked when I called his name for a speaker award that afternoon. He said he did a double take and looked around to make sure there was no one else named Jon from his high school there competing. But the most powerful thing Jon told me was that at that tournament, when adults had to listen to him speak his mind, he felt smart. He had never felt smart before. Let me be clear, Jon was *very* smart. But debate gave him an opportunity to finally feel heard and validated. Jon kept debating and after graduating, he judged and helped at tournaments while he continued his studies. Feeling smart suddenly meant school *was* "his thing."

Jon's story has always stood out to me in my career. Every young person deserves the opportunity to show the world their brilliance. But these stories get crowded out in our noisy world of 24/7 news and millions of Google searches. It is only because of debate that I learned to ask questions and to listen. In fact, to hear Jon's story, I remember sitting in uncomfortable silence as he thought about what he wanted to say on camera. Debate trains you to listen—to *actively* listen. More than just listening to the opposing team, debate also trains you to listen to the judge. Whether through reading a ballot or discussion at the end of a debate, students learn to explore decisions. Win or lose, students look for ways to better present their argument and persuade someone in the future. This is the true art of persuasion. Debaters are not taught just to preach to the choir, but instead to persuade each individual in front of them. This broader application of persuasion often propels alumni of debate to talk about times they have won an argument in front of the seemingly unpersuadable person.

Competing in speech and debate in high school and college was a positively transformative experience. Debate gave me a network of lifelong friends and mentors that pushed me to do better and be better. Ken Strange, legendary Dartmouth College director of debate, taught me that I only got to be disappointed about failure if I had worked hard to succeed. Much of my debate experience was nested within the values of humility, equity, integrity, leadership, respect, and service. Thanks to my debate coaches, my mentors, and my fellow debaters, these core values are part and parcel of my views of interscholastic speech and debate. Debate can be a powerful opportunity to unleash student potential. When debate is grounded in these core values, it not only gives young people the skills to reach for personal excellence, but also gives these students a superpower to create the change they want to occur in their worlds. If our world wants to truly live the ethic of "in it together," our superheroes must come prepared with the skills learned best through the socially just vision of interscholastic debate for which this book argues. Change our world. Start a speech and debate team.

Notes

1. I changed the student's name because this story is his, and I am merely recounting it to the best of my memory.

19.
The Debater

Rashad Howard

I love competing and, for me, competing in debate was a way to become human.

Until age twelve, I lived in and around Los Angeles. I witnessed a lot of police brutality and harassment, but the cops were always Hispanic, Black, *and* white, so I never knew it as *racism*. Many of the neighborhoods I frequented were inhabited by drug dealers and gangbangers. I didn't really view police harassment as much different than I'd get from kids who harassed me with "what set you claim?" or would try to jump me and my friends for being from a different neighborhood, looking at them wrong; taking our belongings; or, because it was Wednesday. Although I view it through the lens of maturity now, I don't remember anything I would have called *racism* from personal experiences. I only understood it through listening to adult conversations, watching TV, or listening to rap music.

When I moved to Arkansas in the summer of 1990, it felt different. I could literally feel "it" in the air. To this day, when I visit the Deep South, upon smelling the air and hearing the crickets, locusts, and katydids chirping on a humid ninety-degree day, I get a sinking feeling in my stomach and it sounds, feels, and smells like racism. The deadly kind. The hangin' by a tree kind. The white mob justifiably chasing and killing you at the behest of a false white female witness kind.

It's in the air. On road trips into the Deep South, I'm still terrified. The sinking feeling has been conditioned. It's my flight response. My warning alarm. That conditioned feeling was deliberately *programmed* during my youth for me to understand and be aware that whatever racism was (*is*), it was definitely and explicitly there to dehumanize me. It was there to convince me and remind me that I was less than. Not just less than white people, but less than human. Those loud ass insects had more rights to the air than me. Their freedom to loudly and constantly proclaim their (Southern) American-ness was an entitlement I recognized was not for me. It reminded me that I didn't, and shouldn't expect, to *feel* equal—or feel that I deserved or had any rights to the heavy air I breathed.

I lived in Fort Smith, Arkansas, at a time when the Ku Klux Klan—a group I'd never heard of until I was twelve—would host rallies and parades in downtown Fort Smith. This is a familiar story I share with millions of others with a legacy that includes being descendants of enslaved Africans, and the progeny of those who lived (and are still living) through Jim Crow laws.

Way Down in Dixie

I attended Southside High School, and my overall experience was a wonderful time of growth and acceptance. I was an excellent student, had a diverse group of friends, and had a great time. It was, however, northwest Arkansas, which still had deep vestiges of racial tension and negative reminders of a dark past vying to remain a relevant present.

My high school was situated on the *southside* of Fort Smith. Our cross-town high school rivalry was Northside High School, which was, of course, situated on the *northside* of town. Fort Smith was fairly homogeneous with a population that was less than 10 percent *Black* and close to 80 percent *white*.[1] Northside was known as the Black school, mostly because a disproportionate number of their athletes were Black—even though the Black student population itself was close to the same 10 percent as the city.[2] Conversely, when I graduated from Southside in 1996, I was one of three Black graduates I can remember in a class of about five hundred.

When the two teams played football, everyone was a stakeholder. The team you cheered for had a lot to do with which high school you or your children attended, but also had a lot to do with what political, sociological, cultural, and historical context you supported. I wanted to go to Northside, but I lived on the southside. Also, my mother was adamant I receive the best "exposure" possible to educational opportunities, resources, and (white) people who would prepare me for the "real world" where white people were in charge. My mother was also an optimist, who, spending most of her adulthood in Los Angeles didn't sympathize or identify as deeply with the contexts I regularly encountered, nor did she want me growing up myopically segregating myself with those with whom I was particularly comfortable: more Black people.

Our high school mascot was *Johnny Reb*. When you entered the front doors, you were greeted by a large statue of Johnny Reb, the national symbol of the Confederacy.[3] You stepped into a time capsule into Dixieland.

In fact, my high school's official fight song was *Confederate Song— I Wish I Was in Dixieland* ("Dixie" for short). Many of the Southside Rebels' students and fans attended high school games with Confederate flags waving from their cars, even though the Confederate flag was (officially) banned from school property. Nevertheless, the banners they drew for players to run through at the beginning of home games always featured a caricature of Johnny Reb in his Confederate uniform and the Confederate flag somehow weaved into the image.

I still have pep rally t-shirts from the time that prominently featured the Confederate flag. I recall the football team might have had one or two Black players, and that our basketball team had five or six Black players (including myself). I also recall us proudly breaking through the Johnny Reb banners before our games as the crowd enthusiastically cheered this procession, clapping in unison to the trumpets blaring the "I wish I was in Dixie" melody.

Whenever we played Northside in basketball, the energy of the town was as intense as Gettysburg. Supporters of each team came in the building ready to direct their lifetimes of either fighting oppression (activism) or justifying subjugation and segregation (oppression) at the children on the court. Winning and losing for either side was personal for every fan. It was an indictment on life. It was heritage.

When Northside won, Black people felt vindicated. They felt seen. They felt a sense of shared victory similar to the way we felt when O. J. Simpson was found "not guilty" by a jury of his peers. In that moment, the North won the Civil War, enslaved people were free to till the land, and Black people proved to be superior at *something*. The right team won. The Union had prevailed. In those days, I didn't get to feel like the other Black residents in my town. I felt shame.

I was also on the court when we won. As time wound down and it became apparent we would win, the Southside faithful would cheer "The South Shall Rise Again!" to taunt the Northside fans and teams. (*Classmates even proudly displayed* Johnny Reb The South Will Rise Again! *license plates that are still sold to this day.*[4]) I remember being excited to hear this chant, because it meant victory for my team. We would exhort the crowd to continue the chant and would often participate in unison, arms waving in encouragement and fists pumping in delight.

In the same moments, however, the celebrations felt strange. I was sometimes sophisticated enough to understand the looks on the Black faces of Northside fans. I was happy to win the game but felt like a traitor. I couldn't help but see myself as independently and publicly "cooning" for the white man. I saw myself as an *Uncle Tom*[5] or, more appropriately, a *Stephen,*[6] directing my talents toward the protection and upkeep of white power. I was an enslaved person conscripted for the Confederate army. These were the larger contexts on display, such that I couldn't fully enjoy the wins. I was thrilled to win but felt like I'd let all those Black families down. I'd let my race down. My feelings were layered. At the end of the evening when the adrenaline wore off and I laid in my bed contemplating each play from earlier in the evening, I felt an emotional and psychological shift. The shame set in.

While I received accolades as an athlete, I felt that complimenting my physical abilities was confirming white supremacy. It validated the racism. The compliments never came for my intelligence, as it rarely does for Black athletes, even when my athletic successes came from being a more intelligent player. I felt what I've heard described as *white gaze*, where I perceived a collective sentiment summed up by this statement that I heard from otherwise well-meaning white friends in Arkansas: "Well, of course you're great at sports. You're Black. You were made for that. Black people are always the best athletes." That was the additional layer I believed some Southside fans secretly felt when they beat the Black school. They were validated that they had the *intelligence* to accomplish what would otherwise be physically impossible—and were yet again "all-around supreme."

I'm more adept at explaining my complex emotions today than I was at the time. In those days I was angry. I seethed inside at the consistent reminders of terror and subjugation, while living (and somewhat thriving) in an ecosystem where Black inferiority was, in a way that I couldn't quite grasp, normal, expected. I attended and played sports at a school in which our mascot, symbols, and fight song celebrated the legacy and heritage of slavery—of my ancestors. Of me. I was confused and angry and entirely incapable of expressing it in any meaningful way.

A Different World

Beyond the racism, there were some really bright spots. My best friend was Franqua Bell (who now goes by Coach Q). He dropped seemingly out of nowhere to become one of my biggest inspirations in excellence. A year ahead of me in school and a fellow basketball player, he took me under his wing as an older brother would his younger protégé. When he attended the American Legion's Boys State and was elected governor, I wanted to do the same. Eventually, I had my chance.

My second day at Boys State, I met Khalid Reede Jones. He was a skinny kid with a high-top fade (like Kid from Kid 'n Play), had glasses, wore Timberland boots, and carried himself with a swag and confidence totally unlike the Southern kids I was normally around. He had a slight New York accent and a way of making witty and funny comments about everything happening around us. He was also really loud. All the time. His speech and his words were poignant and aggressive. All the time. Looking back, he was the first kid who was a peer of mine that clearly didn't give a fuck. He wasn't arrogant. He was just—unapologetic. We became fast friends.

We hung out every day, listening to music and reciting rap lyrics in between civics training sessions and mock votes. I was taken by his confidence. It wasn't just the swag, but it was also the way he used words. He would explicate hip hop lyrics like an English teacher and engage in random debates with all the kids at Boys State—*and he always won*. He always had the right analysis, the right words, and depth of understanding to persuade the room.

I found he attended Little Rock Central High School and his only extracurricular activity was Speech and Debate. He talked about debate rounds in which he competed and won on topics like U.S. immigration issues, policing, and racism. He talked about *building cases* and *running disads* that demoralized his opponents. He talked about how he listened to Wu-Tang Clan and Jeru the Damaja before debate rounds to get hyped, then go in and argue someone into submission. I was enthralled.

I never had the command of my words or my emotions the way Khalid did. I'd been a musician and singer for several years but had never known how to use my mouth as an instrument of intellect. I could get people to *feel* what I was saying, but rarely get them to *think* in entirely new ways. I wanted in, and I left Boys State resolute that I would focus on debate. I was at a point in my life where I wanted to say something. *What I wanted to say and how I wanted to say it couldn't be expressed on the basketball court.*

And Franqua had already graduated, so he wouldn't be back to encourage me on the court. A week before classes started my senior year, I called Ms. Joanne Elsken, the Southside drama, speech, and debate teacher to ask if I could join the team. She didn't know who I was (*which I thought was impossible as I was a starter on the basketball team and one of only a few Black kids at the school*) but let me know the counselor needed to add it to my class schedule.

I quit high school sports to debate.

High School Debate

I was more excited than I'd ever been about starting classes and spent the entire first day anxiously anticipating getting to debate class. When I got there, I knew a couple of my classmates and nothing else. I didn't understand the concept of a *resolution*, the order of the affirmative and negative, the concept of *flow*, or even that China, this abstract land of Chinese people, cold temperatures, a big wall, and rice farms had a place called Tiananmen Square. I had no idea before that day that China was considered a communist country and, embarrassingly, was unfamiliar with what would constitute a *human rights* violation.

Our resolution for that year was *Resolved: That the United States government should substantially change its foreign policy toward the People's Republic of China.*

I asked, "Is the People's Republic of China different from regular China?" Sadly, it was an honest question. As the weeks went by, however, I spent most of my afternoons thumbing through *cards* that had been cut out of journal articles and placed in *files*. I learned how to create my own case file, which was nothing more than a small folder of information I carried in a leather briefcase until after I left my first debate tournament having been exposed to how "real" debaters carted around their own file boxes of very well-organized research.

When I left for my first tournament, I watched the varsity debaters loading the bus with a lot of file boxes and carts. I thought nothing of it until we got to the tournament. Everywhere I looked, I saw students with file boxes, rolling them around on carts and dollies. Their brains and everything they'd researched, studied, and thought critically about were in those boxes, clearly displaying the volume and breadth of their intellectual capacity. I can't help but see their boxes of files versus my singular folder in a briefcase as an appropriate metaphor for what was different about all these kids' lives versus mine.

Up to that point in life, I'd been good at everything I tried. I hadn't needed much practice, and certainly didn't need much in the way of study. This was the first time I felt deeply insecure about my talents and abilities. Nothing I witnessed was familiar to me. None of my previous success in sports, school, church, or anything mattered. I didn't feel capable of drawing on anything I'd learned to that point as a crutch to walk me through. I was intimidated and felt paralyzed.

I saw Khalid and his partner in the hallway, each with their carts of research. Seeing him helped me relax a little, but my apparent calm was a facade. *That*, I was used to. I knew how to act cool when I was terrified. I'd developed the ability to *appear*, as opposed to *remain* calm while walking through rival gang neighborhoods throughout Los Angeles. Appearing calm helped me avoid getting jumped when I was ten.

Khalid showed us how to read the tournament bracket to determine the location and start time for our first round, and I walked the halls of the school to our room with the same terrified, yet cool saunter that led me through neighborhoods in South Central L.A. There were no rival gangs to jump me. Only unfamiliar ideas, modes of communicating, and otherwise unassuming kids who I felt could prove my intellectual inferiority. Those kids, and my perceptions of their abilities were considerably more dangerous to me than the Bloods and Crips. I wasn't afraid they'd physically beat me; I was afraid they'd expose me to myself.

My partner, Ryan Watford, was a handsome, red-headed sophomore. He was tall and had an amazing, deep voice. He was charming, polished, and considerably refined for someone only fifteen years old. I was also a tall kid with a deep voice and a lot of charm. We arrived at our room to meet our competition, who were also competing in their very first debate round. When we shook their hands, they let us know how intimidated they were to do this for the first time. We all immediately relaxed, and I found myself reassuring them that they would do just fine. They were all high school sophomores, and I was a senior. I somehow took leadership in the room.

Ryan and I were on the affirmative. I don't remember any of the arguments we made, but I remember my partner and I filling the air with our voices. When he spoke, I could feel the vibrations in my chest. I assumed my voice did the same to him, and I knew our competition, and more importantly the judge, could feel the same. We were confident in our ignorance, but confident, nonetheless. I remember thinking Ryan knew more than I did about the case. I also remember the judge, a woman who was a teacher at a small school in Arkansas, stopped us mid-round to encourage all of us, taking a moment to specifically tell me I had an amazing and "imposing" presence. We won the round and both Ryan and I accumulated a high number of speaker points for the round. I left relieved and energized.

When I saw Khalid in the hallway, he asked, "How'd it go?"

"Easy," I responded as nonchalantly as I could fake. I wanted to appear completely cool. The truth was that I was brimming with both excitement and terror for the next round.

I'd spent much of my life doing things I was afraid to do, but only when I didn't have a choice. Competing as a novice in that tournament was the first time that I can recall deliberately *choosing* to do something that terrified me. I believe Ryan and I ended up losing the next round, but it didn't matter. I'd found a new way to engage the world. I'd found the perfect outlet for my expression. After attending a few of the poetry and prose rounds, as well as competing in extemporaneous speaking that first evening, I'd found a new passion, a new tribe, and a new way to access—me.

All In

When I got back to Southside, I had a new way to spend my afternoons: researching and studying. Building my files. I read academic journals and periodicals, as well as history and current events books I'd never previously had any interest in reading. I went to the school library and read old newspaper articles on microfiche. I learned my way around the school's Lexis-Nexis research software to find information on every topic imaginable about China. I used reams of Xerox paper to copy everything multiple times, for myself and my teammates to cut into cards to build their case files.

I engaged in countless practice rounds with my teammates to understand how it felt to respond to arguments on the fly, then I spent my evenings reading all my team members' flow sheets to comprehend every argument they heard. I deconstructed and reconstructed arguments, and then thought of new questions for my research. I talked to friends at other schools about the cases they were running, as well as what their competitors' arguments against them were. I became consumed with exercising my intellect in the same way I'd previously been consumed with exercising my body for competition. I was suddenly motivated to begin critically reading the assigned texts in my English and history classes to be able to cross-reference historical and literary contexts in debate rounds.

I studied how my teammates took notes. Autumn Ivy (eventually one of my partners at a few tournaments) would flow with different-colored pens. I started doing that. I thought her flow pages looked like art, which helped me organize my thoughts so much better and led me to enjoy reading debates the same way judges read them. I began to see the arguments themselves as artwork that took shape on paper. The shape and content captured in flow also served as a window into how that person thought. I could literally see what their senses captured.

I started participating in plays and musicals at school to add more *drama* to my speaking. By remembering lines, expressions, and blocking, I learned how to captivate an entire room during debate rounds. I participated in anything that could quickly propel me to win debate rounds, extemporaneous speaking awards, and sweepstakes awards at tournaments. I wanted to walk across the stage at the conclusion of every tournament to receive awards and recognition from peers and teachers for being intellectually and artistically gifted. My height, physical speed, hand-eye coordination, physical aggression, and footwork were no longer my tickets to acceptance and admiration, but that which made me *me* was being noticed.

Debate was a competitive pathway for me to learn how to channel my emotions into logical arguments, then express them eloquently such that the feelings and experiences that shaped my perceptions of the world had to finally be heard. I felt vindicated that my competitive participation, regardless of the rounds won and lost, likely caused cognitive dissonance, particularly among the students and administrators in a Southern state where Black boys were at best expected to be great at sports, possibly music, crime, hard labor, and not much else. Further, I was picking up trophies while representing a school whose cultural foundations were supposed to be the benchmark of Southern, Confederate, white supremacy.

Being a debater made me proud. I no longer felt like a traitor corroborating the notion that Black excellence was limited to physical exploits in sports. Even though our entire team would accumulate points from the debate rounds my partners and I won, I knew I was there to represent myself—and I simply *attended* Southside. It gave me an outlet that didn't require me to physically or violently direct my anger at other Black athletes, but to truly channel it in carefully constructed discourses against mostly white competitors. I could simply beat white people at something at which they were supposed to beat me. I daydreamed (*and really hoped*) that many white kids went home and told their racist parents how they lost to me. I felt like a true rebel among "Rebels."

Being a debater allowed me to mute the dog whistle of white supremacy and reprogrammed me so that I had the ability to drown it out—erasing its ability to maintain hold over me.

Being a debater helped me reverse the years of racist programming that caused me to believe I needed to ever *prove* my humanity. It allowed me to vanquish the very notion that I needed to *do* anything to *become* or to be treated as *equal*. Somewhere in the middle of the research, the card cutting, the creation of disads, the winning and the losing, I overcame the need to try to be anything other than myself.

Programming

No human should feel compelled to prove their humanity in any way. However, the pervasiveness of spending your entire life expected to *struggle* and *overcome*; marching, protesting, and watching marches and protests on TV; striving to be the "first Black" fill-in-the-blank; heeding well-meaning advice to work to be "three times better than" your white counterparts at everything just to be regarded as "equal"; being treated like the "exceptional Negro" who is "not like all the other Black people I know" by your white "friends"; being lied to about, then reminded that *your history began with your people as enslaved people*; being schooled in a cultural context that robbed me of any cultural heritage; being psychologically affirmed and emotionally rewarded only for athletic talent; being bombarded by the notion that my only way to experience success in life would be via extraordinary physical exploits in a sports arena; being proselytized to that God made me Black and gave me this Black experience as a curse for Ham; being educated to believe that I should be grateful for slavery because, without it, my "savage ancestors" would never have been introduced to God; being patronized by graven images of Jesus as a white man who would punish me to Hell if I didn't bow down and *give my life to him*; being forced to read passages of Twain's *Huckleberry Finn* in the tenth grade, in class and out loud, where my classmates were encouraged to confidently read *n*—— (over two hundred times) as homage to the literary and historic significance of the book, as well as the period and author's intent; being told to *calm down* every time I defended myself with the same fervor and volume as my non-Black counterparts; being told that Africa is ugly and Africans themselves are ugly and poor people with no relevant contributions to world history, civilizations, human enlightenment, or anything civil; being laughed at by my eighth grade history teacher, and subsequently the rest of my classmates when I told her I wanted to go to Duke University and she told me "you need to be smart to get into that school" and, upon laughing, she permitted my classmates to join in unison; and so on; and still so on; and so on into adulthood. All of this was/has been/is exhausting, and at the time made me feel the need to prove my humanity.[7] I knew being athletic wasn't enough, and likewise believed being smart wasn't enough, especially since my grades didn't inoculate me from being humiliated as if I wasn't intelligent. I needed to also compete at something *smart* to demonstrate, or provide tangible, behavioral evidence of my intelligence. As a debater, *I* was evidence.

Reprogramming

My senior year competing in high school forensics rehabilitated me from my addiction to self-deprecation. It was a recovery process that added tangible coping skills: clear communication, critical thinking, and creative expression. The many, high-pressure cross-examinations taught me how to manage my emotions, particularly when ideas to which I had emotionally tied myself came under intense scrutiny, condescension, and even strategically delivered ad hominem attacks. I experienced what it felt like to have the presence of mind to remain in control of myself and felt liberated from being psychologically bullied by racist tropes and inhuman treatment.

Debate engaged me in my own reprogramming process and my new program served to liberate me. I no longer grasped for self-determination as an abstract yearning but developed a process and practice to apply it in my own life. Debate was my liberating force and gave me the power to decide what to perceive, and how to defend those perceptions. Debate gave me the blueprint to my freedom, as well as the weapons to demand it. Debate gave me power.

College Debate

That power and confidence materialized into an appointment to the United States Air Force Academy (USAFA). After a summer of basic cadet training, where I and about 1,100 classmates endured significant emotional, physical, and psychological challenges, I was excited about rekindling the intellectual challenges debate offered. At the end of the first day of classes I found my way into a small classroom in a corner of Fairchild Hall where the USAFA Forensics team would meet daily to research, practice, receive coaching, construct and review cases, and challenge each other to think differently and openly.

At USAFA, all cadet programs are cadet-led. This meant our actual debate coaches were our team captains and upper-class cadets. As a freshman, my coaches were Shawn Briscoe and Marshall McMullen. The two debate partners were seniors on our team and served as the two principally responsible for our training, endlessly seeking to sharpen our abilities, place in tournaments, and increase our national rankings.

The first time I saw the two of them compete in a practice round against our other upper-class coaches/team members (Luke Savoie and Ryan Sullivan), I knew I had walked into a quite different league and level. As a basketball fan, I've followed NBA players who are asked to describe the difference between playing in high school and college and the NBA. These elite athletes regularly mention *the speed of the game* as the most significant difference, along with the persistent *quality of the athletes*. At those elite levels, every competitor is among the world's best in athletic ability and competitive understanding of the game. For these competitors, they are the best and smartest in the world.

Witnessing the two teams in competition intimidated me to no end. The speed of the first affirmative speaker, *literally the speed* at which he read the case, was astonishing. I couldn't understand or keep pace to effectively flow (take notes) nor to hear and process each argument. The cross-examination questions set up arguments that were, for the moment, more nuanced and complex than I could comprehend. The intensity of the debaters was at an apex, yet all four of the competitors seemed in complete emotional control and unfazed entirely by the brilliant, and (what I perceived as impenetrable) arguments/counterarguments.

Over the next month or so before our first competitive tournament, Shawn and Marshall spent countless hours forcing us deeper into case and disadvantage development. They taught us how to research by simply asking us questions about the arguments we were constructing then countering with off the cuff responses, playing an effective devil's advocate as effortlessly as an encouraging supporter. I don't remember the exact arguments, nor do I particularly remember the resolution (although I believe it had something to do with Southeast Asia). What I do remember is feeling like I couldn't begin thinking about arguments and/or responses until I actually researched enough to become intimately familiar with current U.S. policies; frameworks for policymaking; traditional philosophical and ideological positions; and a bevy of other things that were completely new to me.

College policy debate was an entirely different experience. I was no longer competing to overcome feelings of inferiority or racism but competing among intellectual savants with mutant-level brain processing power and speed. The literal and figurative speed of the game forced me to practice, listen, research, and think rapidly and more profoundly. All the debaters competing at that level were captivating, experienced speakers, so I could no longer rely on height, charm, voice, or anything other than the quality of the arguments my partner and I made, and the clarity with which we were about to convincingly deliver them.

Humanity

I remember cutting cards late one night with my classmates and stopping to reflect on how happy I was. I was conscious that, perhaps for the first time, I was competing in a sport that judged only my arguments and my abilities as close to fairly as I had ever experienced. It was the first time I felt I was truly competing in an activity that was merit and performance based. To win, you had to be good, and everyone was good and could offer feedback on how to be better. It was a true meritocracy, where neither my physical strength nor physical talents could propel me or provide justification for someone to dismiss any of my achievements with *of course you're good at debate—you're Black*! Every win and every loss was something that had to be earned, and in that moment, I knew I was earning it. In that moment, for once, I was no longer questioning my humanity nor was I juggling shame and elation. My brain was preoccupied with simply trying to think, learn, compete, and win in a space where anxiety, triumph, pain, exuberance, disappointment, and victory were all equitably distributed.

Debate is a beautiful sport played with words and ideas. The words and ideas we are constantly constructing and deconstructing, advocating and vilifying in parallel, sharpen our character. The literal process of thinking in debate forces each human to see all sides of the argument, and thus, all sides of the human beings making them. Debate is the pinnacle of human connection, a literal competitive process to both understand and be understood. Debate forces one to be empathetic, engaged, yet calculated and callous (and the spectrum of psychological and emotional states in between that make us human) all in the same moment. I've cried with sadness and with joy over debate. I've shouted with both anger and elation. Competing sometimes left me feeling small and outmatched, intimidated and defeated, as well as confident and encouraged. Debate was literally a safe space that allowed me to know the fullness of what it was like to be, experience, and be regarded as, simply, a human being.

Notes

1. "Fort Smith, Arkansas," City-Data.com, 2021, accessed January 18, 2021, www.city-data.com/city/Fort-Smith-Arkansas.html.

2. "Northside High School," SchoolDigger, 2006–2021, accessed January 18, 2021, https://www.schooldigger.com/go/AR/schools/0633000367/school .aspx#:~:text=Compare%20Details%20Northside%20High%20School%20has %20the%20largest%20high%20school,%2C%20African%20American%20 (11.9%25).&text=Compare%20Details%2078.7%25%20of%20students,a%20 free%20or%20discounted%20lunch.

3. Krystle Sherell, "Southside to Move Johnny Reb Statue in June," KFSM ABC 5 News, accessed January 24, 2021, https://www.5newsonline.com /article/news/local/outreach/back-to-school/southside-to-move-johnny-reb -statue-in-june/527-5ffba422-c4bd-43ff-a7b1-6342082b83a7.

4. "New! The South Shall Rise Again License Plate With Johnny Reb," *WorthPoint*, accessed January 24, 2021, https://www.worthpoint.com /worthopedia/south-shall-rise-again-license-plate-1851414865.

5. The pejorative character reference to a Black man who is warm and protective of his oppressors.

6. The character played by Samuel L. Jackson in Quentin Tarantino's *Django Unchained* not only protects his oppressors but acts on his behalf in the oppression of other enslaved Black people.

7. Duzi Magwaza, "The Psychology of Cruelty," YouTube. Online video clip, accessed July 13, 2021, https://www.youtube.com/watch?v=_P1wIpu0lTc.

Glossary

Bibliography

Contributors

Glossary

Presented here is an alphabetical listing of key words and terms used by debaters in this book.

Aff: Many debaters refer to their affirmative case or affirmative strategy simply as their aff.

cards: Quoted evidence used by debaters. The word is a holdover from the days when debaters physically cut quotations and glued them to index cards.

case: Refers to the story told by the affirmative team during the first affirmative constructive.

CEDA: Cross Examination Debate Association. Originally a breakaway organization from the NDT, by the 1990s it was largely comprised of debaters practicing the progressive style of debate. Nontraditional approaches first took hold here, as well. It is the primary organization promoting policy debate in college and hosts an annual national championship tournament.

constructive: One of the first four speeches in a policy debate when arguments are constructed, explored, and developed.

counterplan: A course of action advocated by the negative team as an alternative to the affirmative plan.

cross-examination: The time following a constructive speech in which the opposing team may ask questions of the speaker. In policy debate, it is usually three minutes in length.

cutting cards: Conducting research and putting it into useful forms that can be accessed later in a debate round. Many years ago, debaters literally cut quotations and pasted them on index cards that were carried in file boxes. Today, the act of cutting cards is completed using the cut and paste functions in word processing software.

disadvantage: *Also DA, disad.* An unintended consequence of an action. It demonstrates that something bad will happen if a plan is passed.

flow: *Also flowing, flows.* The notes of what transpired in a debate round or the act of taking notes. It usually refers to a specialized method of taking notes that allows participants to track the arguments quickly and accurately in a debate as they progress throughout the round.

frontline: The prewritten first line of responses to an opponent's arguments. Debaters often prep frontlines to potential arguments their opponents might make.

kritik: An argument that challenges the assumptions, logic, methodologies, or thought processes present in the round.

line-by-line: The point-for-point discussion of an argument. When viewing the flow of a debate round, one can see the various lines of argument that occurred. Using the line-by-line refers to examining each line of argument in turn.

NAUDL: National Association for Urban Debate Leagues. A national-level nonprofit that provides support to city urban debate leagues. It hosts an annual urban debate national championship.

NDCA: National Debate Coaches Association. An organization that supports high school coaches and debaters.

NDT: National Debate Tournament. The organization that hosts the longest-running collegiate policy debate national championship.

NSDA: National Speech and Debate Association. The largest national honor society for middle and high school speech and debate. It is a nonprofit organization that promotes speech and debate, including the largest national championship tournament in the world.

overview: Students sometimes use overviews to frame their argumentative positions in the mind of the judge relative to other arguments and advocacies.

plan: A course of action. In most policy debate rounds, it is a description of a proposed course of action (by the affirmative team) that could be implemented by the United States federal government.

resolution: The broad topic to be debated. It is set by a governing organization such as the NSDA or CEDA.

round: A single matchup between two debate teams. Tournaments consist of multiple preliminary rounds (usually 4, 6, or 8) prior to identifying the top teams that advance to elimination rounds.

signpost: *Also signposting.* Verbally identifying where the speaker is on the flow.

speed: In contemporary debates, students often speak significantly faster than they would in normal conversation. This tactic allows debaters to maximize a precious resource—time—in a debate round.

spreading: Presenting multiple responses to a single argument. The tactic involves presenting a plethora of independent responses so that a debater may have multiple options for defeating an opponent's ideas. It is often, but not necessarily, accompanied with speed. Colloquially, many simply use the term spreading as a substitute for any combination of talking fast and/or giving multiple responses to an argument.

UDL: urban debate league. A non-specific acronym referring to nonprofit organizations that support debate programming and competitions in cities.

uniting the crowns: The achievement of winning both collegiate national policy debate championships within the same year: the NDT and CEDA. This is like winning the Grand Slam in professional tennis or golf.

WDI: Women's Debate Institute. A nonprofit organization devoted to promoting gender-inclusivity in debate.

Bibliography

Achen, Christopher, and Larry Bartels. *Democracy for Realists: Why Elections Do Not Produce Responsive Government*. Princeton: Princeton University Press, 2016.

Allen, Mike, Sandra Berkowitz, Steve Hunt, and Allan Louden. "Measuring the Impact of Forensics and Communication Education on Critical Thinking: A Meta-analytic Summary." Paper presented at the 83rd annual meeting of the National Communication Association, Chicago, IL, November 19–23, 1997.

Aristotle. *Rhetoric*. Vol. 2 of *The Works of Aristotle*, translated by W. Rhys Roberts, 593–680. Chicago: Encyclopaedia Britannica, 1993.

———. *The Nicomachean Ethics*. Translated by J. A. K. Thomson. London: Penguin Books, 2004.

Bilyeu, Bob. "An Army of One, A Challenge to Debate Coaches." *Rostrum*, April 2004.

Bond, Shannon. "Just 12 People Are Behind Most Vaccine Hoaxes on Social Media, Research Shows." *NPR*, May 14, 2021, accessed August 4, 2021, https://www.npr.org/2021/05/13/996570855 /disinformation-dozen-test-facebooks-twitters-ability-to-curb -vaccine-hoaxes.

Briscoe, Shawn F. "Forensics: A Socio-Emotional Learning Space." *Rostrum* 83, no. 4, December 2008.

———. "Forensics: Enhancing Civic Literacy and Democracy." *Principal Leadership*, May 2009.

———. *Why Debate: Transformed by Academic Discourse*. My Debate Resources, 2016.

City-Data.com. "Fort Smith, Arkansas." 2021, accessed January 18, 2021, www.city-data.com/city/Fort-Smith-Arkansas.html.

Come Clean. Performed by Jeru the Damaja. By Kendrick Jeru Davis, Kirk Jones, Shelly Manne, Chris E. Martin, Fred Scruggs, and Tyrone Taylor. Produced by DJ Premier. Payday Records, 1993.

Debate Team. Directed by B. Douglas Robbins. Green Lamp Pictures in association with Long Strand Studios, 2008. DVD.

Deutschendorf, Harvey. "7 Reasons Why Emotional Intelligence Is One of the Fastest-Growing Job Skills." *Fast Company*, May 4, 2016, accessed January 21, 2021, https://www.fastcompany.com/3059481 /7-reasons-why-emotional-intelligence-is-one-of-the-fastest -growing-job-skills#:~:text=According%20to%20the%20 World%20Economic,been%20growing%20in%20recent %20years.

Dillard, Coshandra. "The Weaponization of Whiteness in Schools: It's Time to Recognize and Stop the Pattern." *Teaching Tolerance* 65, Fall 2020, np. https://www.tolerance.org/magazine/fall-2020 /the-weaponization-of-whiteness-in-schools?fbclid=IwAR37 fDLFRLICWc8QGHWKqHJGIYHJ8ivYusr0qviZy43W3E7i30 LY1y91PRk.

Dillard-Knox, Tiffany Yvonne. "Against the Grain: The Challenges of Black Discourse within Intercollegiate Policy Debate." Master's thesis, University of Louisville, 2014. *Electronic Theses and Dissertations*, paper 2161, 2014. https://doi.org/10.18297/etd/2161.

Dizikes, Peter. "Study: On Twitter, False News Travels Faster than True Stories." *MIT News*, March 8, 2018, accessed August 4, 2021, https:// news.mit.edu/2018/study-twitter-false-news-travels-faster-true -stories-0308.

Dreher, Rod. "How To Speak Gibberish and Win a National Title." *The American Conservative*, May 10, 2014, accessed September 1, 2020, https://www.theamericanconservative.com/dreher/how-to-speak -gibberish-win-a-national-debate-title/.

Economist. "The New Ideology of Race: And What Is Wrong with It," July 9, 2020, accessed August 17, 2020, https://www.economist .com/leaders/2020/07/09/the-new-ideology-of-race.

Educating for American Democracy. "Our Vision." About Us. 2021, accessed August 4, 2021, https://www.educatingforamericand emocracy.org/our-vision/.

Employment Connection. "Homepage," 2020, accessed June 23, 2021, https://www.employmentstl.org/.

Gangel, Jamie, Kevin Liptak, Michael Warren, and Marshall Cohen. "New Details about Trump-McCarthy Shouting Match Show Trump Refused to Call Off the Rioters." *CNN*, February 12, 2021, accessed August 4, 2021, https://www.cnn.com/2021/02/12/politics /trump-mccarthy-shouting-match-details/index.html.

Gray, Alex. "The 10 Skills You Need to Thrive in the Fourth Industrial Revolution." *World Economic Forum*, January 19, 2016, accessed January 21, 2021, https://www.weforum.org/agenda/2016/01/the-10 -skills-you-need-to-thrive-in-the-fourth-industrial-revolution/.

Gray, Emma. "Competitive Debaters Are Ready for Their 'Me Too' Moment." *HuffPost*, October 1, 2020, accessed October 15, 2020, https://www.huffpost.com/entry/high-school-debate-me-too_n _5f7217fcc5b6f622a0c2ab94.

Harper's Magazine. "A Letter on Justice and Open Debate," July 7, 2020, accessed August 17, 2020, https://harpers.org/a-letter-on-justice -and-open-debate/.

Hayes, Chris, and Davey Alba. "Your Local Disinformation." *Why Is This Happening?* Podcast audio, December 8, 2020, https://www .stitcher.com/show/why-is-this-happening-with-chris-hayes /episode/your-local-disinformation-with-davey-alba-200215015.

Heidt, Jenny. "Performance Debates: How to Defend Yourself." *Rostrum*, April 2003, accessed May 25, 2020, https://debate.uvm.edu/NFL /rostrumlib/cxHeidtcx0403.pdf

Henderson, George. *Our Souls to Keep: Black/White Relations in America.* Yarmouth, ME: Intercultural Press, Inc., 1999.

Hensley, Willie. "Speech by Willie Hensley at Bilingual Conference." Speech in Anchorage, AK, February 1981, accessed November 29, 2020, www.alaskool.org/native-Ed/2hensley1.html.

Herb, Jeremy, Ryan Nobles, and Dana Bash. "Republicans Keep Their Distance from Matt Gaetz." *CNN*, April 6, 2021, accessed August 4, 2021, https://www.cnn.com/2021/04/06/politics/matt-gaetz -republican-reaction-congress/index.html.

Institute for Speech and Debate. "Angelique Ronald," no date, accessed October 15, 2020, https://ispeechanddebate.com/faculties /angelique-ronald/.

Jiggins, Janice. *Changing the Boundaries: Women-Centered Perspectives on Populations and the Environment.* Washington, D.C.: Island Press, 1994.

Johnson, E. Patrick. "'Quare' Studies, or (Almost) Everything I Know about Queer Studies I learned from My Grandmother." *Text and Performance Quarterly* 21, no. 1 (2001): 1–25. http://dx.doi.org /10.1080/10462930128119.

Klein, Ezra. "How Democracies Die, Explained: The Problems in American Democracy Run Far Deeper than Trump." Vox, February 2, 2018, accessed August 4, 2021, https://www.vox.com/policy-and -politics/2018/2/2/16929764/how-democracies-die-trump-book -levitsky-ziblatt.

———. *Why We're Polarized*. New York: Avid Reader Press, 2020.

Lepore, Jill. *If Then: How the Simulmatics Corporation Invented the Future*. New York: W.W. Norton and Company, 2020.

Levitsky, Steven, and Daniel Ziblatt. *How Democracies Die*. New York: Penguin Random House Publishing, 2018.

Licheva, Zornista. "Why Emotional Intelligence Is a Top 10 Skill." *Access MBA*, February 21, 2020, accessed January 21, 2021, https://www. accessmba.com/articles/view/why-emotional-intelligence-is-a-top -10-skill.

Marquette, Chris. "McCarthy Has 'No' Regrets Opposing Jan. 6 Independent Commission: GOP Leader Opposes Select Committee As Well." *Roll Call*, June 25, 2021, accessed August 4, 2021, "https:// www.rollcall.com/2021/06/25/mccarthy-has-no-regrets-opposing -jan-6-independent-commission/.

Martin, Judith N., and Thomas K. Nakayama. *Intercultural Communication in Contexts*. Boston, MA: McGraw-Hill, 2004.

Mezuk, Briana, Irina Bondarenko, Suzanne Smith, and Eric Tucker. "Impact of Participating in a Policy Debate Program on Academic Achievement: Evidence from the Chicago Urban Debate League." *Educational Research and Reviews* 6, no. 9, September 5, 2011, 622–35, https://urbandebate.org/download/5/why-it-matters/335 /journal-of-adolescence-mezuk-et-al.pdf.

Magwaza, Duzi. "The Psychology of Cruelty." YouTube. Online video clip, accessed July 13, 2021, https://www.youtube.com/watch?v =_P1wIpu01Tc.

Mill, John Stuart. *On Liberty*. United Kingdom: Project Gutenberg, 1859, https://www.gutenberg.org/files/34901/34901-h/34901-h.htm, United Kingdom: Project Gutenberg, January 10, 2011.

————. *On Liberty*. 1869. *Classics of Moral and Political Theory*. Edited by Michael L. Morgan, 1044–1115. Indianapolis, IN: Hackett Publishing Company, 1992.

National Speech and Debate Association. "Ella Schnake 'Debate Like a Girl'—Program Oral Interpretation Champion—Nationals 2019." YouTube. Online video clip, accessed October 15, 2020, https://www.youtube.com/watch?v=Ii5HtExwEDc.

National Symposium for Debate. "Emporia State University Makes Collegiate Policy Debate History." *NSD Update*, April 2, 2013. http://nsdupdate.com/2013/emporia-state-university-makes-collegiate-policy-debate-history-wins-ndt-and-ceda/.

Ogles, Jacob. "Poll Finds Majority of GOP Voters in Matt Gaetz's District Still Stand with Him." *Florida Politics*, April 11, 2021, accessed August 4, 2021, https://floridapolitics.com/archives/419120-poll-finds-majority-of-republicans-in-matt-gaetzs-home-district-stand-with-him/.

Olasiji, Thompson Dele. "Intercultural Dimensions." Lectures presented for Human Relations 5110–108: International Human Relations, University of Oklahoma, Hurlburt Field, FL, July 12–14, 2004.

O'Rourke, Dan. "Policy Debate Is Committing Rhetorical Suicide: Let's Save Lincoln Douglas." *Rostrum*, December 2009.

Palmer, Parker J. *The Courage to Teach*. San Francisco, CA: Jossey-Bass, 1998.

Petrone, Paul. "The Skills Companies Need Most in 2019—And How to Learn Them." *Linkedin*, January 1, 2019, accessed August 3, 2020, https://www.linkedin.com/pulse/skills-companies-need-most-2019-how-learn-them-paul-petrone#:~:text=The%20Hard%20Skills%20Companies%20Need%20Most%20in%202019, . . . %205%20UX%20Design.%20 . . . %20More%20items . . . %20.

Plato. *Republic*. Translated by G. M. A. Grube. *Classics of Moral and Political Theory*, edited by Michael L. Morgan, 31–231. Indianapolis, IN: Hackett Publishing Company, 1992.

Rabinow, Paul, and Nicholas Rose, eds. *The Essential Foucault: Selections from the Essential Works of Foucault, 1954–1984*. New York: The New Press, 2003.

Reid-Brinkley, Shanara Rose. "Ghetto Kids Gone Good: Race, Representation, and Authority in the Scripting of Inner-City Youths in the

Urban Debate League." *Argumentation and Advocacy* 49, no. 2, February 2, 2017, 77–99. https://doi.org/10.1080/00028533.2012 .11821781

———. *Voice Dipped in Black: The Louisville Project and the Birth of Black Radical Argument in College Policy Debate*. Oxford: Oxford University Press, 2019.

Rocket Science. Directed by Jeffrey Blitz. B&W Films, Duly Noted, HBO Films, and Rocket Science Inc., 2007. DVD.

SchoolDigger. "Northside High School." 2006–2021, accessed January 18, 2021, https://www.schooldigger.com/go/AR/schools/0633000367 /school.aspx#:~:text=Compare%20Details%20Northside%20High %20School%20has%20the%20largest%20high%20school,%2C%20 African%20American%20(11.9%25).&text=Compare%20Details %2078.7%25%20of%20students,a%20free%20or%20discounted %20lunch.

Sciullo, Nick J. "The Racial Coding of Performance Debate: Race, Difference, and Policy Debate." *Argumentation and Advocacy* 55, no. 4, October 12, 2019, 303–321. DOI: 10.1080/10511431.2019.1672028.

Shackelford, Daniel. "The BUDL Effect: Examining Academic Achievement and Engagement Outcomes of Preadolescent Baltimore Urban Debate League Participants." Paper for the National Association for Urban Debate Leagues, 2019, https://urbandebate.org /download/5/why-it-matters/338/the-budl-effect.pdf.

Sherell, Krystle. "Southside to Move Johnny Reb Statue in June." *KFSM ABC 5 News*, accessed January 24, 2021, https://www.5newsonline .com/article/news/local/outreach/back-to-school/southside-to -move-johnny-reb-statue-in-june/527–5ffba422-c4bd-43ff-a7b1 –6342082b83a7.

Sizer, Theodore R., and Nancy Faust Sizer. *The Students Are Watching: Schools and the Moral Contract*. Boston, MA: Beacon Press, 1999.

Sorkin, Amy Davidson. "The G.O.P.'s Matt Gaetz Problem." *New Yorker*, April 11, 2021, accessed August 4, 2021, https://www.newyorker .com/magazine/2021/04/19/the-gops-matt-gaetz-problem.

Statt, Nick. "Major Tech Platforms Say They're 'Jointly Combating Fraud and Misinformation' about COVID-19." *The Verge*, March 16, 2020, accessed August 4, 2021, https://www.theverge.com/2020/3/16 /21182726/coronavirus-covid-19-facebook-google-twitter-youtube -joint-effort-misinformation-fraud.

Stirgus, Eric. "Morehouse Team Pulled Out of Debate Competition, Citing Racist Taunts." *Atlanta Journal Constitution*, April 29, 2021, https://www.ajc.com/education/morehouse-team-pulled-out-of -debate-competition-citing-racist-taunts/VUDNY3ZILFHMDN YOKYP43DYINU/.

TalentSmartEQ. "Homepage," 2020, accessed February 6, 2021, https::// www.talentsmarteq.com.

Tyone, Mary. Ttheek'and Ut'iin Yaaniida' Qqnign': Old-time Stories of the Scottie Creek People. Transcribed and edited by James Kari. Fairbanks, AK: Alaska Native Language Center and Mary Tyone, 1996.

Warmbrodt, Zachary. "'Most Influential Voice': Warren's Network Spreads throughout Biden Administration." *Politico*, March 15, 2021, accessed August 4, 2021, https://www.politico.com/news/2021 /03/15/elizabeth-warren-aides-biden-administration-475653.

Warren, Elizabeth. *Persist*. New York: Metropolitan Books, 2021.

Women's Debate Institute. "Mission and Story," no date, accessed October 15, 2020, https://womensdebateinstitute.org/.

WorthPoint. "New! The South Shall Rise Again License Plate with Johnny Reb," accessed January 24, 2021, https://www.worthpoint.com /worthopedia/south-shall-rise-again-license-plate-1851414865.

Contributors

ALEX BERRY is a graduate of Tulane University of New Orleans, majoring in political science and communication. He works in the Tenants' Rights Unit at Southeast Louisiana Legal Services and also at the Louisiana Children's Museum. While at Tulane, he served as the president of the Tulane Parliamentary Debate Team and still enjoys staying involved with high school debate in Louisiana.

SHAWN F. BRISCOE is the assistant director of debate at the University of Alaska Anchorage and the state-wide coordinator for drama, debate, and forensics in Alaska. He was a 1998 CEDA All-America debater while attending the United States Air Force Academy. As a proud military spouse (who delights in bucking gender norms), Shawn has had the pleasure of working in a variety of contexts with a diverse population of students who have earned awards at local, regional, national, and international competitions, including at the national championships (high school and college) and the World Universities Debating Championships. His previous texts include the *Companion Guide for Speech and Debate Coaches* and *Policy Debate: A Guide for High School and College Debaters.*

JAMAL BURNS is a first-generation college student and graduate of Duke University, where he majored in history and minored in education. His thesis focused on the often-violent social inscription American public schools attach to the Black boy body by looking through the lens of gender, sexuality, and sociohistorical institution. A 2021 Rhodes Scholar, he attends graduate school at Oxford University.

BENJAMIN COLLINGER is an MBA candidate and dean's fellow at Indiana University's Kelley School of Business. He was previously an associate with Next Street, a national advisory firm advancing equitable economic development and small business growth. As a Venture for America alum of Cleveland, he managed a collective impact partnership to support minority-owned business during the coronavirus pandemic. He graduated magna cum laude from Trinity University with a degree in international studies and history.

NYA FIFER is a former debater from the Collegiate School of Medicine and Bioscience in Saint Louis. Nya qualified for the national tournament of the NAUDL twice and became a part of the top ten debate teams in the league. She served as co-captain of the team. In 2023, she graduated with a degree in biology from Washington University in Saint Louis.

DESIREE HILL debated at McKinley Classical Leadership Academy in Saint Louis. She was also on the volleyball, cheer, and soccer teams, while working after school. Desiree later debated at the University of Kansas (KU). Due to the lack of financial resources Desiree left KU. She now works full-time at a hospital and is preparing to enlist in the navy.

RASHAD HOWARD is an entrepreneur and investor based in Washington, D.C. and San Jose, Costa Rica. His slogan, *business is my activism*, is an expression of creating and building communities where self-determination is a basic way of life. He mentors entrepreneurs to recognize success comes from being the best versions of themselves. He earned a B.S. in English from the United States Air Force Academy and an MBA from Virginia Tech.

GINA IBERRI-SHEA is the director of forensics at the United States Air Force Academy. She has taught and coached intercollegiate debate for over twenty years. She has coached nationally and internationally successful teams in multiple debate formats and has taught debate in several countries for both competitive and language development programs.

SEAN LUECHTEFELD is vice president of membership and communications for American Network of Community Options and Resources and adjunct professor in the master's in communication program at Johns Hopkins University. He earned his PhD in communication with a concentration in rhetoric and political culture from the University of Maryland. He holds a master's degree in communication from Wake Forest University and dual bachelor's degrees in political science and communication studies from Florida State University.

MAYA MCGREGORY debated at McKinley Classical Leadership Academy in Saint Louis Public Schools (SLPS). She participated in the Early College Academy (ECA) at Saint Louis Community College, earning her associate degree while still in high school. Maya is an undergraduate at the University of Kansas (KU), majoring in international business-marketing.

Yari L. Mitchell is president of Y Factor Consulting, Inc. She entered college and the world of collegiate debate at the College of Eastern Utah. Eventually, she took a scholarship for debate and transferred to the University of Miami in Florida where she earned her BA in economics with a minor in mathematics.

Nicole D. Nave debated for the Saint Louis UDL. She became the first Black woman to win both the NDT and CEDA. She was also the first Black woman to win the NDT. Upon graduating from Rutgers University-Newark with a degree in nonprofit organizations and public administration, Nicole became the executive director of the WDI. Nicole earned her master's degree in communication at Baylor University.

Paul Ongtooguk (Inupiaq) is the retired director of Alaska Native Studies at the University of Alaska Anchorage. He was a Gordon Russell Visiting Professor at Dartmouth College, a visiting lecturer at the University of Pennsylvania, and a professor at Illisagvik College for the North Slope of Alaska. He graduated from high school in Nome, Alaska, and received his BA in religion and philosophy at Northwest University and a BA in history from the University of Washington. He received an MA in education from Michigan State University. His father, Tommy Ongtooguk (Inupiaq), was born in Teller, Alaska, and his grandfather, also Inupiaq, was born on Little Diomede Island. Both volunteered and served in the Alaska Territorial Guard.

Pulgeenok Methanie Ongtooguk was born in Kotzebue, Alaska, and is the daughter of Paul Ongtooguk. She enjoys the many forms stories take and has previously published essays and poetry. She especially loves telling old stories and creating new stories to illustrate the world and the people in it for her three kids. She is finishing a degree in social work, psychology, and Alaska Native Studies at the University of Alaska Fairbanks.

Ravi Rao developed a passion for social justice at Washington University in Saint Louis. After completing his legal studies at Chicago-Kent College of Law, he cofounded and directed the Saint Louis UDL. Eventually, he pursued a career in nonprofit fundraising. Ravi lives with his beautiful wife, Kelli, and son/boss Arjuna.

Sara B. Sanchez is responsible for national volunteer engagement and public debate initiatives at the NAUDL. She coached debate at Rowland Hall St. Mark's Upper School in Salt Lake City, Lexington High School in Massachusetts, and Glenbrook South High School in Illinois. Sara has been a classroom teacher, a research analyst at the Utah Foundation, and managing director for Educators 4 Excellence. Sara has a bachelor's in political science from the University of Utah. She writes about baseball for SBNation and BaseballHQ in addition to hosting podcasts about the Cubs and fantasy baseball at Fans First Sports Network.

AUBREY SEMPLE is a teacher and coach for Success Academy High School for the Liberal Arts in New York City and is a board member for Association of Black Argumentation Professionals. Aubrey previously served as the program director for the New York City UDL, founded the Christencher Institute of Vocational Training School, earned the 2015 PASEsetter award for teaching, and is an alumnus of the New York UDL.

ASHLEY SNOOKES earned a BS in political science from Brigham Young University Idaho and an MA in international security and development at Swansea University in the United Kingdom. Ashley is currently the programs manager at Spruce Root Inc., where she is the economic development catalyst for the Sustainable Southeast Partnership. She coaches debate for Thunder Mountain High School.

TARA L. TATE teaches social studies and is the former director of debate at Glenbrook South High School in Illinois as well as several high school and college programs. Her debaters have won numerous state and national championships. She has served in various leadership positions in the NDCA, Northern Illinois District of the NSDA, the Illinois High School Association, the NSDA, and the NFHS.

NICOLE WANZER-SERRANO serves as the NSDA's director of development. She earned her bachelor's in international relations from Dartmouth College. As the executive director of the Dallas Urban Debate Alliance, the league was recognized as the 2012 UDL of the Year. As codirector of the Debate Institutes at Dartmouth, Nicole was awarded the Bronx Science Achievement Award. She was the 2021 recipient of the Thomas Glenn Pelham Award in recognition of devotion to the forensics arts, which teach motivation, integrity, and character.